Pupils with Complex Learning Difficulties: promoting learning using visual materials and methods

by

Jill Porter & Rob Ashdown

A NASEN Publication

Published in 2002

© Jill Porter & Rob Ashdown

ISBN 1 901485 33 1

Published by NASEN.
NASEN is a registered charity. Charity No. 1007023.
NASEN is a company limited by guarantee, registered in England and Wales.
Company No. 2674379.

Further copies of this book and details of NASEN's many other publications may be obtained from the NASEN Bookshop at its registered office:
NASEN House, 4/5 Amber Business Village, Amber Close, Amington, Tamworth, Staffs, B77 4RP.
Tel: 01827 311500 Fax: 01827 313005 Email: welcome@nasen.org.uk
Website: www.nasen.org.uk

Cover design by Raphael Design.
Typeset by J. C. Typesetting.
Typeset in Times and printed in the United Kingdom by Stowes (Stoke-on-Trent).

PUPILS WITH COMPLEX LEARNING DIFFICULTIES: PROMOTING LEARNING USING VISUAL MATERIALS AND METHODS

Contents

Acknowledgements

We would like to thank those colleagues who have helped to formulate our ideas about the use of visual materials and visual methods in teaching. The following people who work at St Luke's School deserve special mention: Peter Binnington, Jenny Burnett, Kay Chappell, Jo Lawson, Sandra Mineham and Heather Newsum. Also thanks are due to Dorothy Smith for her ongoing support and to Luke Ashdown for giving up precious holiday time to do the line drawings.

Chapter 1: Introduction

In this book we explore a number of different teaching methods which have one shared characteristic – they use the visual medium to access learning. We consider the use of signs and symbols for communication, the role of visual perception in understanding about number, learning to read and environments with heightened visual cues. The common feature of these is that they present material visually rather than verbally. In a climate where teachers are often being instructed to use oral methods to promote learning it is particularly important to have an understanding of how we can support learners in other ways.

Which learners are we referring to as having complex needs? We use this term to describe pupils who have moderate, severe or profound learning difficulties in recognition that many may also share a number of learning characteristics with those described as having autistic spectrum disorder (ASD). This is a wide and varied group of learners. They include pupils who do not simply require a differentiated curriculum or teaching at a slower pace but who at times require further adaptations to teaching if they are to make progress. As the reader will see, we draw on approaches that have originally been developed with the needs of children with single and dual sensory loss, ASD, as well as learning difficulties. These learners form a heterogeneous group and we are not proposing recipes for intervention. Indeed, teachers are encouraged to use this book to ask themselves questions about their own teaching approaches for particular individuals and to consider whether alternative methods may be more appropriate.

In the past educationalists have tended to be polarised in their views on the use of teaching methods, belonging to distinct and opposite camps, often with heated debates about the strengths and limitations of different approaches. Typically, arguments concerned whether to use behavioural approaches or interactive approaches, adopt child-centred or subject-centred approaches, and promote learning by discovery or use error-free methods of learning. Today we are more likely to recognise that there is no single model of learning that will account for the acquisition of all skills, knowledge and understanding. It is inappropriate to consider that a single teaching approach is all that is required. Rather, it is important that teachers have a whole repertoire of different approaches to draw on, depending on what they are trying to teach and the way pupils respond. This is mirrored in the book with highly structured approaches used in some approaches (see Chapter 7) while the early stages of learning about quantity or numerosity (see Chapter 9) are likely to be more child-centred, building on and developing the interests, games and routines of the individual pupil.

Ann Lewis and Brahm Norwich review the literature asking whether there are specialist pedagogies or teaching approaches that are specific to pupils with special educational needs (SEN) and whether these are related to particular differences between learners. They put forward the idea of continua of teaching approaches, series of adaptations which are used to differing degrees:

'The concept of a continuum implies that there are differences of degree, so by teaching continua we mean that various strategies and procedures which make up teaching can be considered in terms of whether they are more or less used in practice.'

(Lewis & Norwich, 2000, p.56)

As we will see, the research evidence does not unequivocally point to the success of particular methods with identified groups of learners. Time and again reviews of research come to the conclusion that there is a lack of scientific evidence. If we adopt the idea of a continuum with teachers making additional adaptations to differing degrees, then we need to start from an acknowledgement of what constitutes effective teaching generally. Lewis and Norwich provide a useful summary, including the following features.

- clarity about the purposes
- reviewing previous learning
- continuity across teaching sessions
- clear lesson presentations
- teaching in small explicit steps
- attention to feedback to the learner and of the learner's feedback to the teacher
- teacher modelling of 'thinking aloud'
- encouraging pupils to also reflect aloud
- sound subject knowledge
- positive expectations of pupils
- monitoring pupils' attention
- anticipating disruption
- maximising learning time
- flexibility in the choice of teaching strategy

Figure 1.1: Characteristics of effective teaching. (Adapted from Lewis & Norwich, 2000)

Teachers should also be aware of a number of general learning difficulties that pupils may encounter. According to Julie Dockrell and John McShane, these often include:

- difficulty remembering new information;
- [difficulty] in generalising what they have learnt to new situations;
- great difficulty in understanding complex or abstract ideas;
- finish their work more slowly and not complete tasks.

(Dockrell & McShane, 1992, p.171)

Clearly this has implications for the way we teach, suggesting more time to mastery, more opportunities to apply their learning in a range of contexts and complex material presented in a way that enables pupils to build up their understanding a stage at a time. There is a danger that we ascribe these difficulties only to particular groups of learners but, if we take a moment, we may easily identify with these problems ourselves depending on the learning context that we face.

A useful analogy has been made between teaching and driving a car, which we can draw on here: when the learning task is easy we coast along happily in fourth or even fifth gear; however, when the situation changes, we have to apply increasing amounts of attention and we change down gear to have more control over the car. Thus, in a teaching situation we may draw on the principles of effective teaching, if we are experienced, with 'monitoring' levels of attention because practice is almost automatic. However, when our teaching is ineffective in a particular situation, we have to be more reflective in our teaching and draw on additional strategies, often ones that give us greater control over the learning situation.

In the next chapter we will look more closely at the rationale for using visual access methods. The important point here is to demonstrate that it is not our intention to suggest that every learner with complex needs will benefit from the methods included in this book. For example, we know that infants are very sensitive to sound and to movement and pupils at the very earliest stages of development may well respond to other forms of input. Equally, other learners may have difficulty taking in information visually. We know that the rate of visual impairment, including cortical visual impairment, is higher among this group of pupils than in the mainstream population. Therefore we describe and illustrate these approaches with the aim that they will add to the teacher's repertoire.

In the following chapters we discuss different aspects of learning and illustrate the use of visually mediated learning within these. A particular focus is those areas of learning that in themselves facilitate access across curriculum areas, namely communication, reading and numeracy. We also consider the importance of organising and managing the learning environment including the use of multisensory environments. Perhaps, however, the most important chapter is the last one in which we consider ways in which we can evaluate our teaching approaches. Our final chapter of the book is, therefore, designed to enable teachers to reflect on their teaching experiences and to evaluate how successful different approaches have been for individual learners.

Key summary points
- This book concerns approaches to teaching that capitalise on using visual rather than oral methods of teaching.
- They must be seen within the context of general principles for effective teaching.
- They are not presented as a recipe nor a panacea for all pupils, indeed their use must be carefully evaluated.
- They form part of a repertoire of teaching strategies for teachers to draw on.

References and useful further reading
Dockrell, J. & McShane, J. (1992) *Children's Learning Difficulties: A Cognitive Approach.* Oxford: Blackwell.

Lewis, A. & Norwich, B. (2000) *Mapping a Technology for Special Educational Needs.* University of Exeter and University of Warwick.

Norwich, B. & Lewis, A. (2000) 'Mapping a Pedagogy for Special Educational Needs', *British Educational Research Journal*, 27, 3, 313–29.

Chapter 2: Why use visual access methods?

Before we consider specific methods, it is important to examine the rationale underpinning the use of visual rather than oral methods. If we understand why these methods may be more successful, we can ensure that when we use them our practices are consistent and we do not mistakenly minimise their possible impact through inappropriate use. We start by looking at the role of vision and how vision develops in young children. This, of course, is only part of the story. While the eye may be capable of seeing, the brain is responsible for perceiving similarities and differences and, as the child develops, is able to extract meaning and to encode and store information in memory. We then reflect on this in the light of research studies of pupils with learning difficulties.

Vision is a powerful sense, central in enabling us to take in information from the environment, to make sense of our world. Humans have developed to depend heavily on vision with more than half the brain taken up with visual processing. Psychologists have developed theories of cognitive development based on these early perceptual abilities. While all the senses have an important role to play, the distant senses of hearing and vision play a crucial part in the developmental process. During the first year of life vision becomes an increasingly dominant modality through which to take in information about the world. Infants develop their ability to detect form, movement, pattern and colour.

Visual ability depends on the nature of the stimuli, including how interesting they are to the child. It is increasingly recognised that while typically developing infants do not see as well as adults this depends at least in part on the nature of the stimuli. For example, infants are more interested in moving than static stimuli either because the object itself is in motion or the infant. (This explains in part why so many infants and young children respond well to being taken out in the car or wheeled around in a pushchair.) Moving objects attract young children's attention and it is more likely to be sustained attention if the object has particular relevance or meaning for the child. Vision, therefore, has a central role in learning and also develops very early. This suggests that it is a robust source of information.

If we look at development in children without vision we realise the full significance of vision for all-round development. Young children who are blind, for example, are delayed in relation to early understandings in cognition because of the way visual information provides important cues for developing an idea of the permanence of objects. There is a knock-on effect in relation to movement where infant skills of locomotion are delayed until they realise that there is something out there of interest even when they can not hear it or touch it and this provides an *incentive* to crawl.

Indeed, studies of early development on pre-verbal infants with either visual impairment or hearing impairment suggest that visual stimulation plays a more critical role than auditory stimulation. Without vision children lack seeing others use gestures and they do not see others pointing so that opportunities to share meaning with the caregiver are lost. Therefore, children have no clear reference point for understanding what others are talking about, and they cannot easily build up an understanding of the world through the language of others. Research has also revealed that children with a visual impairment are delayed in the development of pretend play and the idea of treating an object symbolically. Again, this has an impact on the development of language.

Why use visual systems?
We have already discussed how robust the early visual system can be and its significant role in development (while also recognising the impact of a visual impairment). As a child develops, language becomes an increasingly important source of information and usually a child starts to rely less heavily on visual information for learning. Memory processes reflect this as children

organise and remember knowledge about the world semantically. However, for many pupils with complex needs the development of language, as a basis for organising, analysing and storing information, is not well developed and, therefore, they continue to rely more heavily on visual modes for learning.

A considerable body of research has focused on identifying particular difficulties that are associated with specific genetic syndromes. The area is fraught with difficulties as researchers have often looked at the profile of particular etiological groups (most notably children with Down syndrome) and largely ignored complexities of genetic expression and the impact of home and environment, to name but a few contributing factors. It is with these considerations in mind that we consider briefly research on youngsters with the most common genetic causes of learning difficulty, Down syndrome and Fragile X. However, we do so while warning the reader of the dangers of stereotyping particular youngsters and seeing the impairment before the child. Nevertheless, the research (while largely ignoring individual variations) reveals a picture of children for whom language is a particular area of difficulty.

In children with Down syndrome, the lag in the development of communication and language cannot be purely accounted for by the increased incidence of hearing impairment. While a fluctuating hearing loss must play a part, the difficulty with language has been linked, in part, to that of poor auditory short-term memory– a difficulty in remembering information that is presented verbally. Visual memory, in contrast, is revealed as an area of relative strength. Therefore, methods have been sought that use visual stimuli such as reading, signs and symbols as a way of aiding language development. The reasons include the fact that visual input of this kind 'lasts longer' than the auditory equivalent. Indeed, for symbols and print, the stimuli can be attended to as long as the person requires. Prolonged presentation does not result in distorting the input in the way that a sustained oral input would do.

Research with children with Down syndrome suggests that they have long attention spans and are less distractible than typically developing infants of the same age and are more visually attentive. However, this may reflect a delay in the development of selective attention where the child is able to 'disengage' from some aspects and direct attention to others. Therefore, they may appear to be fixated on a particular aspect. The ability to provide a sustainable input may be quite important in giving pupils sufficient time to respond.

The rationale for utilising a visual mode of input can, therefore, be linked to particular auditory deficits (as for example a hearing loss), or difficulty encoding auditory information, or to the need for a longer time to respond.

Fragile X is the second largest genetic cause of learning difficulty, so named as it results from a fragile site on the X chromosome. It is less readily recognised as any physical characteristics are more subtle. Research on children with Fragile X suggests that they also have weaknesses in sequential processing, particularly in relation to auditory material, and respond better to visually presented information. Sequential processing is important for solving problems bit by bit in a temporal or serial order, a skill that underlies many academic tasks, and usually these instructions are presented orally rather than in a sequence of pictures or diagrams. Visually presented material may therefore better support their learning.

This section would not be complete without reference to pupils with autistic spectrum disorders, for whom problems with communication form one of a triad of impairments. For these learners a range of intervention strategies have been suggested but one of the most popular is TEACCH, a highly structured, almost asocial approach in which visual programmes guide the youngster with autism to becoming an independent learner. The approach is often used in part with visual timetables and visual clues (e.g. pictures, photographs, symbols, etc.) supporting learning. While a highly popular approach, concerns have been expressed that the learner may become dependent on this 'autistic' approach to learning, if the methods are used too exclusively.

Learning style

Our rationale for thinking about visually mediated learning has, so far, largely concentrated on particular learning difficulties of children with complex needs. We turn back in this section to considering *all* pupils. Research has identified differences in preferred learning style within the mainstream population. One continuum describes learners as 'verbalisers' or 'imagers', as thinking in words or mental pictures. Learners are divided further into those who process information as a whole (often referred to as wholists) and those who process it in parts (the analysts). This has further relevance to considering our teaching approach. Does it assume that the child is best able to take in information step by step or as a whole, in pictorial form or verbally? It would appear that a person's preferred learning style does not necessarily fully reflect his or her relative strengths. Thus, while a pupil with severe learning difficulties may seem quite vocal they may process information better when it is accompanied by signs and symbols.

Conclusion

In this chapter we have outlined a rationale for thinking about the way in which we present information to aid learning. We have made a particular case for being aware of the need of some pupils to access learning visually, rather than orally. These systems may be particularly pertinent for pupils with particular learning difficulties. Additionally it may be a preferred learning style for others. We have, however, also stressed individuality. We draw your attention to these approaches – but not as a panacea for all pupils.

Key summary points
- Vision is the most important sense in relation to development and learning.
- Visual processes develop early.
- The impact of blindness on *early* development provides evidence of the central role of vision in relation to all aspects of early development.
- There is evidence that in a number of pupils with learning difficulties visual processing is *relatively* less impaired than auditory processing.
- A number of teaching approaches are based on the premise that visual approaches may support children's learning not least because they provide relatively static material that can be absorbed over a greater length of time than auditory material.
- Given the diverse needs of pupils with complex disabilities and lack of certainty in any element of current research, it is important that teachers evaluate the methods they use in relation to individual responses.

References and useful further reading

Babbage, R., Byers, R. & Redding, H. (1999) *Approaches to Teaching and Learning: Including Pupils with Learning Difficulties.* London: David Fulton Publishers.

Buckley, S. & Bird, G. (Eds) (2001) *Down Syndrome Issues and Information Education and Development Series.* Portsmouth: Down Syndrome Educational Trust.

Jordan, R. (1999) *Autistic Spectrum Disorder: an introductory handbook for practitioners.* London: David Fulton Publishers.

Chapter 3: Language and communication

There is not the space here to launch into a full description of the development of language and communication in children or the range of language and communication disorders which children can have. If you want to pursue these matters in detail, there are many books to which you may refer and some are listed at the end of this short chapter. However, the focus of this book is very much on language and communication and ways of promoting language development and enabling communication for children with learning difficulties. Therefore, we will first make plain the distinction between language and communication in the belief that this will help you recognise better the relative strengths and needs of children in these areas. This is essential if you are going to determine what you may do as their teacher.

Communication implies that there is one person who sends a message and at least one other person who receives it. Both individuals need to be able to understand the meanings being communicated. Of course, communication does not consist just of one simple exchange of a message; typically strings of messages are communicated rapidly with the individuals swapping roles as the receiver and the sender; and communication exchanges may involve more than just two individuals. Furthermore, communication can be seen as often involving the negotiation of meaning and, therefore, involves a process of clarifying and extending what is 'said', drawing on tone of voice, gestures and other cues. As teachers we need to be examining some ways of enabling children to communicate better in a wider range of ways, with a wider range of people and in a wider range of contexts.

Language is used by us in order to communicate better. If we were not capable of using and understanding a language, we would be dependent solely on basic sounds, actions and body language to communicate. A language consists of a set of quite arbitrary sound sequences, each of which stands for a particular idea or concept by mutual agreement among the group of people who share our particular language. These sound sequences are recognised as words and there are all sorts of accepted rules for stringing together the words to form sentences. Words may be spoken but ideas and concepts may also be represented by signs, pictures and writing. Thus, language is a highly formalised and conventional system which allows us to use specific, but arbitrary, symbols to stand for ideas and concepts and to be combined to express an infinite number of meanings. Indeed, although we have referred to sounds and words, a language can be based around other sorts of symbols.

Children's development can deviate from the normal pattern of development in terms of learning a language and/or learning to communicate. In the normal course of things communication grows out of interactions between caregiver and infant. Adults focus on the sounds and actions the child is making and respond to them as if the child was intentionally communicating. As mother and child become increasingly sensitised to each other and share joint attention, interactive sequences are built up into a kind of turn taking. The infant learns that his or her sounds and actions can have an impact on others and in so doing acquires one of the cornerstones of communication. The infant's responses start to be intentional, responding in a particular way with an expectation of what will happen as a consequence. This responsiveness leads to adults building more elaborate sequences and play routines. As the infant becomes increasingly interested in objects, this shared attention shifts towards incorporating the outside world and in so doing creates a number of additional reasons to communicate. There are a number of good texts that describe the purposes of communication, from the earliest where the child communicates to use another person to gain something or uses an action to gain joint attention, through to the more sophisticated uses of communication to pretend, to provoke and to tease.

This very brief description of early communicative development starts to alert us to some of the difficulties children may encounter and why it may be necessary to teach even these early skills. For a number of reasons this early social interaction, including the development of shared (and enjoyable) attention, may not be experienced. The outside world including other people may be of limited interest to the child. As a consequence, they may not have learnt that, if they act intentionally it will have a particular effect on others. Alternatively they may have acquired this understanding but only with respect to behaviours that serve to reduce interaction and further opportunities to communicate. As we will see in later chapters, this means that for some children the approach to teaching may have to be structured around the things that do interest them and about which they are most likely to want to communicate.

Children may also experience disorders and delays of language, for example, disorders of language form, content or use. Disorders of form may include phonological difficulties (e.g. a reduced or unusual system of sounds, poor sound discrimination) and syntactic difficulties (e.g. problems with sequencing words in sentences). Disorders of content can arise, for example, from having a limited fund of ideas and concepts, word finding difficulties and general difficulties in learning new concepts and the associated words. Disorders of use can be many: for instance, difficulties in understanding the needs and preferences of listeners can lead to children talking interminably on topics that interest nobody but themselves or failing to give crucial information that aids understanding. Children may be limited in the ways in which they use their language to communicate.

A full discussion of these matters can be found in John Harris's book on research into early childhood language development and the implications of research findings for intervention programmes. What we need to note in particular here is that the origins of language and communication difficulties do not necessarily lie with problems in the children alone; communication is after all a two-way process. As their teachers, we have the ability and the knowledge to compensate for any difficulties that they have and open the way for the development of meaningful communication with them. In various ways people may have failed, through lack of knowledge or awareness, to encourage them or to teach them the skills that they require. Indeed, there is much evidence that the communication skills of children with quite profound difficulties can be improved as a direct result of changing the nature of the communication environment that we provide for them. Children do not suddenly begin to communicate by magic, although the process often seems magical. In the case of all children, including those without learning difficulties, adults have typically had to work hard to achieve this: they have gone out of their way to encourage children to become involved in interactions with them; they have done their best to interpret children's actions and speech, even when there may have been no real communicative intent; and they have responded immediately and appropriately to children's communication acts in a way that encourages them to communicate better and more often.

The language used by teachers can provide formidable barriers to learning for many young children. Basically, the language used at school can be very different from that at home and can be used in very different ways. In particular, the language of teachers contains proportionately more questions to check for understanding and instructions. Also, the classroom environment and activities are highly controlled by teachers. The result can be that there are fewer opportunities for the children to make spontaneous contributions and to initiate interactions and activities at school than they do at home. This means that there can be less of the talk between children and between children and adults which is essential for their social, conceptual and language development. The practical difficulty for teachers who wish to encourage more contributions and questions from children, is that they have to relax the reins somewhat so that the children can be more physically active and engage in a greater range of activities with their peers. They have to be flexible in their planning and find ways of recognising and responding to the exchanges initiated by children through their comments and questions.

There are a number of ways in which teachers can assist children with language and communication difficulties. Better attending and listening may be facilitated by using meaningful and interesting activities, and by getting the children's attention before giving any instructions or asking questions. Some children simply may not respond when instructions are given to the whole class or group, because they may not appreciate that they are intended for them too. In such cases, always call the child's name and gain eye contact before giving instructions. Also, it helps if background noise and other distractions within the environment can be kept to a minimum, because some children with auditory problems have great difficulty in screening out irrelevant noises and focusing on your words. Comprehension may be facilitated by such little acts as checking that a child's spectacles are not caked with grime or that a hearing aid is operating properly. It is very important to know the child's level of understanding of spoken words: it is surprising how many children come into school not knowing vocabulary that we all take for granted and use extensively as teachers. Your instructions or questions or explanations should match the child's level of understanding: avoid long and complex utterances; support what you say with meaningful gestures; break down what you say into shorter sequences; check all the time for signs that you are understood; if you are unsure whether the child understands you, get him or her to repeat what you have said; be prepared to repeat what you have said or rephrase it; be concise and explicit; avoid sarcasm or idioms which children do not usually understand and which may add to their confusion; and, wherever possible, establish clear routines which will aid children's understanding of what they have to do. Expression should be encouraged whenever children attempt to communicate their ideas, feelings or lack of understanding; be seen to be listening to what they say; give the children sufficient time to respond; model alternative ways of expressing what the child communicates; and give the children opportunities to engage in activities that positively encourage interactions with their peers.

For many children with learning difficulties, teachers will have to modify their language even more drastically. Indeed, with children with autism and severe learning difficulties, it has been suggested that the spoken language used must be a bare minimum and that there should be a far greater emphasis on the use of visual methods (modelling, demonstration, physical guidance) and visual languages (use of pictures and signs) to instruct and inform. In essence, the argument is that these children have major problems when processing spoken language, but they have many strengths when it comes to processing information that is presented visually. Of course, this is not necessarily true of all children with learning difficulties, but it is these visual methods that are explored in the following chapters. It should be noted, however, that modifying our language should not reduce our interaction with a pupil, nor should it limit the types of *way* in which we use communication. If we want children to understand that communication can be used for a whole range of different purposes, we need to ensure that we provide an appropriate model, we do not only communicate to them by giving instructions.

Choice of visual system
It is worth just briefly discussing alternative and augmentative systems of communication and the differences between them. Visual systems of communication are many and varied – typically, they employ manual signs, objects, photos, pictures, stylised pictures (usually called symbols in this book) and/or the written word. The systems can be 'low tech', employing at most boards or books containing pictures, photos or symbols, or they can be 'high tech', involving use of a range of information and communication technology in speech-producing machines of various kinds. For some children, there will be a lifelong reliance on these visual systems of communication and they are used effectively as an alternative to speech because comprehension and production of speech is impossible. For most children, however, these visual systems are used as augmentative systems – they are used while the children are learning to communicate better through the spoken word, mainly as an additional aid to the listener. They should also be

used by teachers and others when they communicate with the children because they have difficulties in understanding spoken language. Ideally, all visual systems would be regarded as augmentative systems, because use and understanding of the spoken language without any prompts should be the ultimate goal. In practice, elements of visual language systems will continue to be useful even with those children who have relatively good speech skills.

The type of visual system chosen for a particular child is a crucial matter. It depends upon making careful judgements about their relative advantages and disadvantages.

Who will share the systems with the child? How easy is it to learn? How readily is it understood by naïve listeners? Does the child have the physical and/or intellectual ability? What kind of supportive environment is required to foster the child's spontaneous use of the system? How much equipment has to be carried around and does this create problems of accessibility? The choices made at this stage by others can have a profound effect upon children's development – people will decide for them what system they will learn and when and where they can use it.

The approaches to developing communication described in the following text largely use either objects or pictorial symbols. In practice, a range of media have been used. For instance, in their short practical guide Eve and Neil Jackson show how photography may be used to improve the understanding of people with learning difficulties. Some children may well be able to cope with the printed word instead of pictures. Typically, writers have suggested that there may be a developmental progression that is broadly, with some variations, as follows:

1. actual objects;
2. photos and realistic pictures;
3. more stylised pictures and line drawings (and, perhaps, miniature representations);
4. pictorial symbols and more abstract symbols;
5. printed word.

It should not be assumed that pupils must necessarily follow this progression. For example, some workers introduce pictorial symbols straightaway and seem to be successful with many children. There is also disagreement about how essential it is to have picture-object, picture-symbol and symbol-word matching activities. To complicate matters, it is clear that, for instance, some symbols in pictorial systems are simpler than others: they range from (1) those symbols that are little more than stylised line drawings of actual objects; to (2) verbs that are depicted using simple stick men; and to (3) other vocabulary that is represented using abstract geometric shapes, dots and directional arrows.

The nature of the materials used inevitably depends upon a careful assessment of each individual child. Thus, the media may be regarded as being at one of four broad levels.

Basic level – Objects are used which can stand for a thing or activity. The object is actually the thing, or is closely associated with it, or features prominently in an activity (e.g. a cup at drinks time). The wrappers for favourite foods might be used. This type of reference material is appropriate for pupils who cannot understand that photos or symbols can represent something else.

Possible intermediate level – Photos of the objects or activities. The items in the photos must still have a close relationship to the thing or activity to which reference is being made. The pictured object should be the actual thing or feature significantly in some way in the activity. Miniatures might also be used. This type of reference material may be appropriate for some pupils, but may not be essential for all.

Advanced level – Pictorial symbols will be used in the first instance. These will probably be taken from one of the symbol systems which are readily available. These symbols are easily drawn freehand but, increasingly, teachers are using software produced for computers which includes massive banks of thousands of symbols. Ultimately, children may respond to the printed word alone, so the printed word may be combined with the symbols. Photos may be necessary for depicting family members and other significant people. This material will be appropriate to the majority of pupils, probably.

Final level – The printed word only. However, symbols or pictures can be literally embedded in words to provide additional prompts to word recognition for pupils with learning difficulties.

The choice of communication depends upon conducting a thorough assessment of the child's strengths and needs. For instance, the child should respond to a variety of visual stimuli if it is intended to teach communication by signs or symbols. Teaching of signing may not fare well if the pupil has poor control over arm and hand movements – a symbol system may be useful instead. There are a number of decisions that must be made and they are best made in consultation with the child's family, a speech and language therapist, and support staff in the school. By sharing information and considering the issues surrounding the choice and construction of an appropriate communication system, you will arrive at what is most suitable for the particular children with whom you work. The chapters in this book illustrate a range of systems used with different pupils and it is offered as an informational guide which should assist you in this process.

Key summary points
- Language enables us to communicate very effectively and in many different settings and with many different people.
- Children's development can deviate from the typical pattern of language and communication development in many ways.
- Teachers and others have the means of compensating for any language difficulties that children have and can enable them to communicate better.
- The learning environment must be responsive and tailored to meet children's communication needs.
- Adults must modify their spoken language to suit each child.
- Adults should consider the way in which they use spoken language and give more emphasis to visual language systems.
- There are a variety of alternative and augmentative visual language systems and choice of the appropriate one depends upon a range of factors relating to the child's strengths and needs and their daily living and learning environments.

References and useful further reading

Coupe O'Kane, J. & Goldbart, J. (1998) *Communication Before Speech.* London: David Fulton Publishers.

Dewart, H. & Summers, S. (1995) *The Pragmatics Profile of Everyday Communication Skills in Children.* Windsor: NFER-Nelson.

Dockrell, J. & McShane, J. (1992) *Children's Learning Difficulties.* Oxford: Blackwell. (See Chapter 3 'Specific Difficulties with Language'.)

Harris, J. (1990) *Early Language Development: Implications for Clinical and Educational Practice.* London: Routledge.

Jackson, E. & Jackson, N. (1999) *Learning Disability in Focus: The Use of Photography in the Care of People with a Learning Disability.* London: Jessica Kingsley.

Latham, C. & Miles, A. (2001) *Communication, Culture and Classroom Practice.* London: David Fulton Publishers.

Chapter 4: Informal communication and sign language systems

The use of body language by humans has been the subject of much study by ethologists. For instance, an acclaimed series of books by Desmond Morris shows how widespread the use of visual languages is. In books like *Manwatching* and *The Human Animal*, Morris shows us how we make movements with our hands that reflect our changing moods, how a number of uniquely human facial expressions are embedded into our visual communication systems, how a range of specific hand and arm gestures may assume local meanings but many unconscious actions are understood worldwide, how our body actions reveal what we are thinking and feeling during the course of every social interaction and how we reassure, provide pleasure, communicate needs and inform by our body language. In this chapter, there is a brief survey of the methods used to develop communication through body language and the elaboration of specific, deliberate gestures in sign language systems for children with learning difficulties.

Affective communication

Some children with profound and multiple learning difficulties do not communicate even by the earliest means and are said to be at a stage of pre-intentional communication. However, it is possible for people who know them well to assign meanings to certain emotional responses that suggest enjoyment and dislike of activities and to recognise states of alertness and interest in these children. Judith Coupe O'Kane and Juliet Goldbart describe one approach to establishing intentional communication that they called the 'affective communication method'. The various steps in this teaching approach may be summarised as follows. First of all, a variety of stimuli are presented to the individual child and his or her observable responses to each are noted. These stimuli may be auditory, visual, tactile or olfactory or a complex combination of these, such as human contact, specific sounds, tastes of specific foods, bright disco lights and so on. The child must be given time to respond to each stimulus before presenting the next one and a provisional interpretation of the meaning of the pupil's responses – vocalisations, facial expressions or body actions – has to be made in each case. The next step involves representing those stimuli that produced the child's strongest responses. Checks are made for the consistency of the child's responses and the behaviours that may be interpreted as 'like' or 'dislike' are identified. The final step is to actually teach the child that behaving in certain ways will have an effect on the people who are doing these things to him or her. Situations are set up that are known to evoke specific potentially communicative behaviour, i.e. the behaviour that can be said to communicate emotional reactions to the stimuli. When potentially communicative behaviour has been evoked, the teacher responds to the pupil's behaviour in a relevant and consistent way *as though the child is intentionally communicating*. Therefore, if the child's behaviour indicates 'like', the interesting or pleasing item or activity is presented again. Conversely, if the child's behaviour indicates 'dislike', the item or activity is stopped or withdrawn immediately.

The assumption is that after sufficient experiences of this nature the child will come to realise that he or she can behave in ways that communicate desires or rejection of things or activities. In such interactions are sown the seeds of simple communication and choice making by many children. It is essential, therefore, that children should always be in a position to control and have an effect on their environment and the people in it. Emphasis should always be given to the two-way aspect of communication and a warm, social context must be provided. Jean Ware has stressed the need for responsive environments for such children and emphasised that adults should always:

* respond to children's vocalisations and emotional responses;
* talk about things and events;
* alert children to activities that are about to happen;
* react to and initiate smiling, laughing, etc;

- encourage children to make eye contact when being talked to and to look at objects that are being talked about;
- imitate the children's own vocalisations, actions and facial expressions;
- give the children enough time to respond.

Work by Nicola Grove and her colleagues point to the importance of validating our interpretation of communication. Children's responses are often a subtle configuration that may be made more readily in some settings than others and we must through careful observation check for evidence that we have inferred the meaning correctly.

Informal communication

Many children with severe and complex learning difficulties do learn to communicate but do so rarely and/or in the most basic ways. Some communicate mainly by manipulating people, such as pulling an adult by the hand over to the cupboard where the toys are kept or by taking and placing the adult's hands on a tap in a way that suggests that they want it turned on for a drink of water. Others may attract an adult's attention and use simple gestures, such as pointing to an object that is out of reach or pushing away a proffered item. Such children may not be able to follow even the simplest of instructions from adults unless these are accompanied by gestures or physical prompts and the context is unambiguous. Even so, some may still require physical guidance from an adult to complete an activity before they come to understand what is expected of them in routine situations.

The aim of teaching activities must be (1) to support their existing communication skills and (2) to foster the development of more sophisticated expressive skills. A number of books are available that contain ideas for appropriate teaching activities: again, the book by Judith Coupe O'Kane and Juliet Goldbart gives a good guide. A key step is to identify activities and things that the individual child likes or needs. It is important to allow opportunities for choice and to encourage choosing, since these children will have preferences that they simply have not learned to communicate. It is essential to convey to these children that their actions can obtain from other people all sorts of things that they want or need. This requires careful engineering of situations so that reasons to communicate are set up. If all things are done for them or if they have free access to everything they want, there is no reason to communicate. If they do not know how to gain attention, to ask for things or activities, they have to be taught how to do so using simple actions that they can easily perform. These may be simple gestures, such as touching, pointing to or looking at desired things. These very basic forms of communication may be systematically elicited and encouraged by having items in sight, but just out of reach, which are known to be preferred by children. Most children will reach for the item and are rewarded by the adult giving it. In the fullness of time children can be taught to use this reaching response to 'point' to desired items that are further away and this simple gesture can even be shaped into a deliberate pointing action. Some children, however, may be unable to reach for physical reasons and may have to be taught to indicate their preferences by looking at desired items. Initially, looking may not be a form of intentional communication, but children may realise that it can have this function if they are consistently rewarded by being given the item when they look at it. Children may enjoy particular forms of interaction or activities. Pausing during the course of these can elicit a response from children which can be used as a cue to continue.

Alan did not request items in an obvious way. He could be sat at table with a favourite toy just out of reach and he would say or do nothing, although from time to time he would glance at the toy. His teacher felt that he needed to be shown that he could obtain things that he wanted by pointing to them. Teaching was initially done in a screened-off area of the classroom. A toy, which he was known to enjoy playing with, was put on the table just out of Alan's reach. The teacher physically guided him to reach out in the direction of the toy and then she would say 'Oh. You want the X' and she would give him the toy. Alan would sit and play with the toy with obvious enjoyment. This was done with a number of different toys on different occasions with the teacher gradually fading out her prompt for the reaching response until one day Alan actually reached quite spontaneously in the direction of the toy on the table. Soon, this basic reaching response was firmly established and the teacher began to move the desired toys further and further way from Alan until eventually they were on high shelves or the top of a cupboard, but still in sight. In these situations in the classroom Alan has learned to use a very basic response to exert some control over his teacher to get things he wants. Future steps in teaching will focus on teaching Alan to do this with other people in other places. Also, he will have to be taught some way of getting an adult's attention before using the reaching gesture because, characteristically, he reaches out without looking to see what the adult is doing. Nevertheless, a good start has been made and Alan has learned one way of communicating to his own benefit.

Children may have to be taught various ways of seeking attention from adults by, for example, touching an adult on the arm or vocalising. This very simple form of communication may be developed by physically guiding them to touch the adult and by making sure that pupils are rewarded immediately by interaction with the adult in a pleasurable activity. Some children may show little or no interest in others and there is a need to break down barriers to communication such as withdrawal or avoidance. It must be an aim to increase the amount of interaction between adults and children in the context of activities that are pleasurable for the children. In this way, adults become associated with pleasant feelings and experiences and, thus, become more attractive themselves. It is crucial to the success of communication programmes that they become more socially responsive and such activities provide opportunities to build up social relationships.

At a later stage, teaching may focus on developing the use of gestures to 'label' events. Children may not think to draw the attention of others to things and they may not respond when we try to get them to focus on things happening in their environment. It is important to teach them how to draw attention to objects or events for the sake of sharing these experiences by prompting them and rewarding them for simple gestures that accomplish this. Also, they have to be taught to follow with their eyes an adult's pointing gesture, firstly to near items that are of potential interest and then to items that are at increasingly greater distances from them.

Perhaps surprisingly, many children with profound learning difficulties seem unable to express rejection of things or activities; less surprisingly, some may do so in ways that are wholly unacceptable. A target with these children will be to teach them acceptable ways in which they may use simple gestures to reject adult interference in their activities, or unwanted objects that are offered to them, or activities that they do not like. For instance, pupils may be offered objects that are not liked and then prompted to push them away. Again, it is crucial that adults are responsive to such simple behaviours if the children are to realise their communicative power. Otherwise, they may learn to use a variety of less acceptable behaviours to communicate their needs and wishes. Of course, problems may arise if a child has been taught how to express rejection in an appropriate way and then proceeds to reject all approaches initiated by others. Negative interactions of this nature can only be avoided by consistently developing the range of positive interactions with people and by giving them positive consequences for their attempts to communicate in more acceptable ways.

Sign language systems

It is now considered a logical step to move from teaching simple gestures to teaching the more specific gestures of a sign language system. Sign language systems have become well established in special schools for children with severe learning difficulties and children with autism over the past three decades. These eminently visual languages have been borrowed from the deaf communities in various countries, modified and used successfully with many pupils who have poor communication skills. If taught skilfully, signs may be used in a formal augmentative communication system to break down communication barriers and to make it easier for children to understand new vocabulary and language structures. There has also been much evidence that children's speech develops and improves over time and that this may be attributable to the use of sign language.

Much has been written about the use of sign languages with different groups of children and adults and there is not the space to review the literature here. However, as regards children with communication difficulties who are not deaf, some basic findings are worth summarising. Firstly, and most importantly, speech will not develop 'by magic'. As well as teaching use of signs, teachers must systematically develop children's range and frequency of vocalising, vocal imitation, plus any imitative and spontaneous speech. This is painstaking work and expressive speech skills will be difficult for many children to achieve and beyond the reach of a significant minority. Typically, there are several stages to a 'total communication' approach:

1. The child is taught to comprehend signs paired with speech and is taught to sign.
2. The child is taught to comprehend signs paired with speech and, increasingly speech alone, and is encouraged to use speech with signs.
3. The child is taught to comprehend speech that is not accompanied by signs and is also encouraged to use speech on its own.

In truth, there could be several sub-stages among the ones identified above. Transition from one stage to the next should begin only when a child shows some indication of becoming aware of adult speech (e.g. by looking at the adult talking, looking at the adult's mouth moving) or own use of 'scribble talk' or simpler vocalisations. The stages are not rigidly defined and, inevitably, some backtracking through the stages is necessary when new vocabulary or structures are taught. Even though the teacher should take the cue from the child's behaviour, the emphasis is upon pushing him or her gently forward by increasingly demanding more. This is required to minimise the risk that children only use signs at the expense of learning to speak.

British Sign Language (BSL) is the sign language of the deaf community in the UK. It is a natural language which develops in line with the day-to-day needs of the deaf people who use it. The basic Makaton Vocabulary, which consists of 350 modified signs from BSL, is the most commonly used sign system in British special schools for children with severe learning difficulties. In recent years, additional signs have been added to the vocabulary, and where schools have not found the enlarged Makaton Vocabulary adequate for their needs, they have used additional signs from other available sign language systems or from BSL.

Guidance on the introduction of signing has been of variable quality, although recommendations for good practice have been summarised by Chris Kiernan, Barbara Reid and Juliet Goldbart in training materials for teachers. When communicating with children who are dependent on signs, teachers should use the word order of spoken English and speak the full sentence as they sign, even though they must sign key words only. There is a possibility that this 'sentence-to-key signs' approach may confuse some children if unsigned words are carelessly paired in time with signs which do not refer to them. For instance, in the sentence 'The ball is on the table' the teacher may inadvertently only sign 'ball' and 'table', but in the time it takes to sign 'ball' may say the words 'The ball is on...' and sign 'table' while saying '...the table'. A possible effect of careless signing is that children may focus upon the signs rather than what is said because the signs are more readily decoded and more meaningful. This could hinder rather than help children learn a receptive vocabulary for spoken words. Also, if signs always precede the spoken word or are produced simultaneously, there seems to be no reason why they should focus upon the spoken words and learn their meaning. For these reasons, words should be carefully paired with signs and, as children progress in learning signs, their teachers must fade the signs out. This may be done by delaying giving a sign after saying the word, so that the children are forced to attend to the spoken word. Also, teachers must be careful in their selection of the vocabulary and sentence structures in order to ensure that speech is kept simple enough for children to learn. This may, in itself, facilitate the development of speech in some cases.

Advice can always be obtained from speech therapists and there are no shortages of courses and inexpensive glossaries for signs. These are the reasons why the use of sign language systems has become so firmly established. However, teaching signing is not easy and it has not proved to be a panacea. There can be extreme variability in the number of signs acquired by children, ranging from none, to just a few, to many hundreds. Even when children have learned signs they do not necessarily use them spontaneously. In part, these problems may stem from the quality of teaching, especially when there has been too much emphasis upon teaching children to label things rather than providing frequent opportunities for them to request things they want and exert greater control over their environment, or simply to share attention and communicate about an activity or event that is important to them. In part, it does not help that sign language is not used or understood in most daily living environments. In part, failure may stem from the learning difficulties and styles of children. For instance, children with autism may be no more motivated to communicate by signing than they would be to use any speech skills that they have; prompting and fading procedures can be used to develop essential imitative skills of children with profound learning difficulties, but the process can be slow or non-existent; and many children simply do not have the fine motor coordination skills to perform the actions required for 'articulate' signing. Perhaps it is also highly significant that signs, like spoken words, are ephemeral and demand good memory skills. Learning and remembering signs is easier when they use natural rather than arbitrary gestures – consider the bizarre nature (and origin) of the BSL signs for sugar or biscuit, for instance. However, we must also consider what models we provide as we interact generally with children.

Teaching pupils to use signs has been highly successful with some pupils. Unlike pictures or objects of reference, which are discussed in later chapters, it is not necessary to develop ways of accessing cumbersome communication boards and books when they are needed. A teacher's hands and a child's hands cannot be misplaced and are always there when they are needed. So signs may have an important role to play in developing natural communication. However, it must not be forgotten that signing has its limitations and they have to be borne in mind when working with children who do not effectively process ephemeral information. If children lack supporting skills of memory, fine motor coordination and attention, more positive results may be achievable using concrete items such as objects of reference and pictures, as these place fewer demands on them.

Key summary points
- There are a range of informal and formalised ways of communicating visually using body language, gestures and signs.
- Teachers must identify suitable behaviour on the part of each individual child that can be assigned a communicative meaning such as like/dislike, I want, no.

- Situations often have to be creatively engineered so that this behaviour on the part of the child is consistently evoked.
- Teachers must consistently respond to this behaviour when it is evoked as though the child is intentionally communicating.
- Teachers must ensure that everybody works to create a warm responsive environment in which all attempts by children to communicate are recognised and responded to.
- Teachers must carefully consider the language that they are using when communicating with each child.
- Teachers must ensure they sign key words as they actually speak them so that they are paired in time.
- Teachers must plan how they are going to fade out signs or gestures and encourage vocalisations and speech.

References and useful further reading

Coupe O'Kane, J. & Goldbart, J. (1998) *Communication Before Speech.* London: David Fulton Publishers.

Gompertz, J. (1997) 'Developing Communication: Early Intervention and Augmentative Signing from Birth to Five Years', in M. Fawcus (Ed.) *Children with Learning Difficulties: A Collaborative Approach to their Education and Management.* London: Whurr.

Grove, N., Bunning, K., Porter, J. & Morgan, M. (2000) *See What I Mean: Guidelines to Aid Understanding of Communication by People with Severe and Profound Learning Disabilities.* Kidderminster: British Institute of Learning Disabilities/MENCAP.

Kiernan, C., Reid, B. & Goldbart, J. (1987) *Foundations of Communication and Language: Course Manual.* Manchester: Manchester University Press.

Morris, D. (1997) *Manwatching: A Field Guide to Human Behaviour.* London: Jonathan Cope.

Morris, D. (1994) *The Human Animal: A Personal View of the Human Species.* London: BBC Books.

Walker, M. (1996) *Makaton Core Vocabulary.* Revised edition. Camberley: Makaton Vocabulary Development Project.

Ware, J. (2000) *Creating a Responsive Environment for People with Profound and Multiple Learning Difficulties.* London: David Fulton Publishers.

Chapter 5: Communication with objects of reference

There has been much reported about the development of augmentative communication systems for use by children who do not speak due to their severe impairments. This chapter explains how 'objects of reference' have been used in communication systems with children with multi-sensory impairments and other children with profound and multiple learning difficulties.

Actual objects have been used in communication systems for more than 30 years with deaf-blind children. Adam Ockelford describes how increasingly objects of reference are being used with children with visual impairments who have problems in speaking or understanding spoken language. Objects of reference are objects that stand for something in the same way that the spoken word does. For example, a child who cannot understand or produce the spoken word 'drink', may be able to use a cup, or understand a communication partner using a cup, to express the same idea. In theory, objects of reference may be made to represent anything that words can. Ockelford gives a number of examples of objects of reference and their equivalent words: for instance, 'drink' can be represented by a cup, 'home' by the key to the front door and an actual person by a bracelet worn by that person.

Figure 1: shows three examples of objects of reference: a cup to represent 'drink'; a spoon for 'dinner'; and a stirrup for 'horse riding'. All three objects have an association with the activity to which they refer. In fact, each is an essential feature of the activity.

The object used may form part of what it stands for: for instance, 'ball pool' can be represented by a ball from the ball pool or 'swings' by a piece of chain. Some objects may be an essential feature of the activity: for instance, 'horse riding' may be represented by a stirrup, 'lunch' by a spoon and 'shopping' by a coin. Some objects may not be a physical part or an essential feature but may be closely associated with what they represent: for instance, a particular classroom may be represented by a bell that matches the bell attached to the classroom door. Finally, Ockelford points out there are a number of wholly abstract concepts, such as 'more' or 'finished', which can only be conveyed by using some arbitrary object and that the links between the object and the concept can only be formed by repeated associations: for instance, he gives the examples of a cross and a circle made of wood to represent 'no' and 'yes' respectively.

Children need to develop particular skills if they are going to understand that particular objects can stand for an activity or a place or a person. Children with severe visual impairments have to be able to discriminate the objects by touch. It may help the learning of these discriminations if objects are used that have distinctive smells or sounds associated with the activity, place or person as well. These additional cues will be especially important for children who have physical disabilities that prevent them feeling the objects. Also, the children have to recognise that people are trying to communicate that an object has a special meaning. Finally, they have to remember the particular meaning that an object has.

The way in which the objects of reference are introduced depends very much on the children's level of understanding of spoken language. Ockelford suggests that with some children with good receptive language, it may be possible to explain that presenting a particular object to a communication partner means that the associated thing will be made available immediately. A few opportunities for some children to use an object to communicate in this way may be sufficient to establish the connection. However, many children will not have reached this level of language development. It will be necessary to establish the connection for them by engineering frequent opportunities in which they are taught to hand over or touch an object for the reward of the immediate occurrence of the associated activity or presentation of the thing. Ockelford suggests starting with just one distinctive object that has a direct physical connection with a strong interest or preference of the individual child before introducing more objects of reference.

Katy has profound learning difficulties and a severe visual impairment. However, she is physically able to locate, pick up and manipulate objects. She really likes Coca-Cola. This was an ideal reward for her teacher. One person, the prompter, sat behind Katy and another, the communication partner, sat in front of her at a table. On the table was placed a plastic beaker. The prompter physically guided Katy to reach out and feel for the beaker. He then prompted her to hand it to the communication partner. The latter immediately gave Katy a small amount of Coca-Cola to drink from the beaker. During the course of ten or so opportunities to do this in a 20-minute session, Katy consumed an amount only equivalent to that in a half-full beaker. After a few weeks, the prompter started to reduce gradually the amount of physical guidance given to Katy. Within six weeks, she was able to locate and hand over the beaker without any physical prompts whatsoever.

Certain principles are probably crucial to the success of teaching in this initial stage. Firstly, objects of reference should be as closely linked as possible to the thing that they represent. Thus, a cup for 'drink' or a spoon for 'dinner' have a direct physical connection with the referent. However, a small piece of dry towelling for 'swimming' does not because towels are usually large, damp and enveloping and are used for drying the body after swimming. Secondly, it helps greatly if the referent is something the child really likes such as a favourite toy, food or activity. Ideally, this strong motivator should be something that can be given in small doses so that the child is likely to want more. Anything that produces rapid satiation, that the child rapidly becomes bored with, is of limited use because it may be necessary to engineer a number of communication opportunities in order to convey to the child that he or she may request it. It does not help matters if the referent is not easily accessible; for instance, a child's favourite activity may be horse riding, but a horse is not going to be immediately to hand. Therefore, it follows that when teaching that, say, a plastic ball stands for 'ball pool', teaching should take place right next to the ball pool rather than in a classroom at some distance from it. Next, the object has to have distinctive features which are likely to make it easy to recognise by touch and/or by use of other senses. Finally, plenty of time must be allowed for teaching the meaning of this first object of reference: Ockelford suggests that for some children making the connection may take many months of effort, although some may do so very quickly.

In the case of Katy's communication programme, she had learned a communicative act within six weeks. However, it could not be assumed that she had learned that the beaker represented her favourite drink. From her point of view, finding and handing over the beaker was what she had to do to get her Coca-Cola. In order to grasp the idea of an object of reference, Katy has to learn that handing over a beaker will get her Coca-Cola but handing over another object will not. The next step was to introduce another object which Katy had to learn to discriminate from the beaker. A wooden block was chosen because it was tactilely quite different and Katy had no interest in block building. Both the cup and the brick were placed in front of her. On the few times that she picked up and handed over the wooden block, she was given wooden blocks to play with. She quickly learned to discard the block and searched further to find the cup. It seemed that a simple discrimination had been made.

This stage of discrimination learning can be a real stumbling block for many children and much depends on the teacher's skill and strategies. One possible strategy might be to introduce a second object that stands for something of no interest at all to the child, as in the case of Katy. In theory, the child should come to realise eventually that handing over the wrong object will be followed by the non-preferred thing. When the child consistently hands over the object for the preferred thing or activity, it is obvious that he or she is discriminating between the two objects. Of course, if the second object represents another favourite thing or activity, there is no incentive for the child to discriminate between the two objects: the child wins no matter what gets handed over. Also, it would be impossible to tell whether the child was responding deliberately or purely by chance.

Once the child is able to discriminate between two objects, a third object may be introduced in the same way as the first. Of course, this new object should represent a preferred thing or activity. Again, there would have to be opportunities to discriminate between this object and the object that represents an uninteresting thing or activity. In this way, discrimination of a range of objects of reference may be taught. Ockelford advises that, initially, objects should be chosen that are strongly contrasting in texture, shape and colour (where a child has residual vision). This could help considerably with discrimination learning.

Objects of reference offer exciting possibilities for communication with children with more profound learning difficulties who may not have an actual visual impairment but who have difficulties in interpreting two-dimensional representations such as pictures or photos. However, there has been almost no research into the use of objects of reference with children who do not intentionally communicate and some variation in practice is reported in the little literature that exists. In particular, we need to understand better what factors are crucial in attaching to ordinary objects their special meaning as objects of reference. Keith Park suggests that there are real dangers in using rigidly standardised communication systems which use a specific set of objects to stand for or represent specific activities or things. It simply cannot be assumed that an apparently commonsensical link between an object and the intended referent can be made obvious to each child. For instance, why should a coin stand for 'shopping'? Why not a shopping bag or a purse instead? It may be the case that some children perceive the crucial element of shopping as having a sweet or a ride in a car to the shops rather than the act of making a purchase.

Standardisation in the use of objects of reference is not necessarily a wrong decision, but Park argues that children who are operating at a pre-intentional communication level need a communication system that is highly individualised and appropriate to their idiosyncratic understanding of their world. One child's set of objects simply may not be appropriate for another.

Park outlines a possible developmental framework for objects of reference in terms of the 'distance' between the objects of reference and their referents. A first step is to use a real object which is actually used in the activity (e.g. a cup identical to the one used for a drink). A next step could be to mount the object on a card so that there is a clear distinction between the object of reference and the actual object (e.g. some raisins glued to a card and the raisins that will be eaten). Other types of objects of reference are at a somewhat greater distance from their referents: an associated object (e.g. a coin to represent 'shopping'); a partial object (e.g. the buckle from a seat belt to represent 'going on the bus'); and an object with one or more shared features (e.g. a piece of vinyl material to represent 'soft play'). Truly arbitrary objects represent the most advanced and most demanding use of objects of reference as symbols (e.g. a wooden circle to represent 'yes'). Some use has also been made of miniatures of real objects (e.g. a small cup to represent 'drink'), but Ockelford notes that there are dangers in using miniatures with children with visual impairments because a miniature has little or no tactile resemblance to the real thing. Thus, using the buckle from a seat belt to represent 'going on the bus' may have much more resemblance to the real thing for some children than a small model minibus, or a few leaves from a tree may be more meaningful than a miniature plastic tree. Park notes that similar considerations may apply to children with profound learning difficulties who cannot make the association between a miniature and the life-sized object.

There are other considerations besides in constructing a communication system, such as the size of the objects, their arrangement and their accessibility. However, when choosing which early objects of reference to teach, the most important consideration relates to what Park calls the 'MMF principle', where MMF stands for Meaningful, Motivating and Frequent. Are the objects of reference, and the concepts to which they refer, meaningful and relevant to the learner? The next consideration when choosing which objects of reference to teach first is whether they relate to highly enjoyable activities or interesting things. Use of an object of reference by the child should give him or her access to an intensely rewarding activity or thing straightaway. What is motivating will vary from child to child. Painting or going for a walk may be definite highlights in the day for one child; for another child the only things that really matter may be food or drink. Incidentally, Park asks why so many people are keen to establish an object of reference for 'toilet' in the early stages. Regrettably, many children with profound learning difficulties do not seem to be highly interested in the toilet and probably do not appreciate the benefits of remaining clean and dry. Therefore, 'toilet' should not be one of the first objects of reference to be taught, even though it is an important one to introduce at a later stage. The final consideration when choosing what to teach is whether there are frequent opportunities to establish the meaning of the object of reference. If swimming occurs only once a week, it is not going to be easy to assign a meaning to the object no matter how much the child enjoys swimming. However, if there is a daily romp in the ball pool, this object of reference may be a better one to teach in the early stages.

When the special meaning of objects of reference has been firmly established, a number of new developments may be pursued. One useful target would be to encourage decision-making. For instance, at snack time a choice of two objects may be offered representing two types of drink or a drink and a biscuit and the children are encouraged to select one. Similarly, it may be possible to offer a choice of activity, such as choosing for a particular song to be sung from several songs. Ockelford suggests that another development could be to gradually increase the amount of time between a child indicating the object of reference and having access to its referent. This way it becomes possible eventually for the child to request the 'ball pool' and be taken from the classroom to go to it. As long as the delay is not too long, it seems reasonable that children should learn that the things they want are not always instantly accessible. As we shall see later, teachers must have a strategy for dealing with the difficult problem that arises when a child requests items that simply are not available.

Key summary points

- Objects of reference are a potential communication tool for children with profound learning difficulties.
- Establishing an object as an object of reference requires careful teaching.
- The link between the object and its referent has to be made clear to the child and it helps if there is a logical link between the two.
- What makes for a good object of reference for any one referent can vary from child to child and it is difficult to impose a standardised system of objects of reference.
- Use of an object of reference by a child should be followed by immediate access to the referent and adults must be highly responsive to communication attempts.
- There should be repeated opportunities to learn the significance of an object of reference.

References and useful further reading

Ockelford, A. (1994) *Objects of Reference.* London: RNIB.

Park, K. (1997) 'How do objects become objects of reference?' *British Journal of Special Education,* 24 (3), 108–14.

Chapter 6: Using pictures to communicate

This chapter provides an overview of the use of pictures in a communication system using the specific example of the Picture Exchange Communication System (PECS), which was developed in Delaware by Andrew Bondy and Lori Frost for use with young children with autism with marked communication and social impairments.

Traditionally, picture-based communication systems have required children to express meanings by pointing to pictures and this has often (though not always) been preceded by much work on teaching the children to match objects to objects, objects to pictures, pictures to objects and so on. Typically, there is also a heavy emphasis on teaching children to respond to requests such as 'Show me the cup.' In contrast, the PECS eschews this traditional approach.

The model for PECS is derived from a behaviourist model of learning and communication. The starting point is to teach children to give a picture of a desired item in exchange for the item. Generally, the pictures used are standard 2-inch square pictures from one of the commercial pictorial symbol sets. Requesting is taught in the early stages because it gives immediate access to activities and things that are highly motivating. Labelling is not regarded as a good language function to teach in the early stages of intervention to children with autism because the only rewards that can be given tend to be social ones which have very weak or no reinforcement effects with such children.

The first phase of the PECS approach with any child is to teach him or her to make the exchange that forms the communicative act. By the end of this phase, the child should be able to pick up a single picture, usually from a tabletop, and put it into the hand of a person in order to get a desired thing. Emphasis is placed on having a good knowledge of what a child's preferences are. When it has been decided what things the child likes, pictures representing each item are got ready. The pictures are representational and small, typically mounted on card and laminated. The approach to teaching the child to make picture exchanges is simple. The picture to be selected is placed on the table in front of the child. The 'communication partner' puts the desired object in full view, perhaps holding it up for the child to see. When he or she naturally begins to reach for it, a 'physical prompter' physically guides the child to pick up the picture and release it into the communication partner's outstretched hand. As soon as this has been done, the communication partner gives the child the reward and says something like, 'You want the ball. Here it is.' The child is given time to enjoy the reward and then the whole sequence is repeated. The communication partner does not refer to the exchange itself by saying something like 'Good. You gave me the picture.' Instead, the adult responds only to the picture exchange as though the child had simply spoken the request. If the child loses interest in that particular item, another picture and the related item is introduced instead. In any case, the teaching session should be terminated when the child shows signs of tiring of the activity.

Observations of Michael and interviews with his parents suggested to his teacher that his main motivators were a particular brand of crisps and certain types of chocolate bar. The use of food rewards is something to be avoided if possible, but they were the only way through to Michael. Therefore, pictures representing crisps and the different sweets were got ready. The pictures were coloured to give an additional cue, mounted on card and laminated. Teaching began using the crisps. Michael and his teacher sat on the floor in a relatively quiet area of the classroom. The teaching assistant was not available to be the prompter because she was managing the rest of the class group. The picture of the crisps was placed on the floor in front of Michael. His teacher held up the packet of crisps for Michael to see and he immediately made a grab for the packet. At this point, his teacher gently took his outstretched hand and guided him to pick up the picture and put it into her outstretched hand. Then she gave him one crisp from the packet saying, 'You want a crisp. Here's a crisp.' Michael ate the crisp, of course. Then, the whole sequence was repeated many times in many sessions. Whenever Michael's teacher felt that he was losing interest in the crisps, she introduced another picture and a favourite sweet instead. After about three weeks, Michael had learned to pick up the picture and hand it over to get his favourite food. However, it should be noted that he was not yet discriminating between the pictures at this stage.

An essential element of teaching is to give the child what he or she wants every time that a picture exchange is made. Of course, this would not necessarily happen in the natural world, but in later phases of teaching the child can be taught to wait for desired things or accept that what is wanted simply is not available. To deny access to a requested thing in this early phase would send out confusing messages to the child. Also, the picture exchange must be initiated by the child, albeit with guidance initially. Therefore, the child is not told to pick up or hand over the picture. Verbal prompts are avoided because there is evidence that children may become prompt-dependent in their learning. Moreover, the child is only physically prompted to make the picture exchange at the point when he or she reaches out towards the desired item, thus initiating the communication act. This physical guidance is faded over time, starting with fading dropping the picture into the communication partner's outstretched hand. Once the child is reliably picking up the picture and putting it into the communication partner's hand, the open-hand cue is also faded. The communication partner waits increasingly longer before holding out his or her hand for the picture and this should force the child to seek actively to place the picture in the partner's hand as would be necessary in a natural environment. Modifications to the prompting strategies may be required if the communication partner does not have an assistant, but the above points must be kept in mind.

The second phase in the PECS approach involves teaching the child to make the communication exchange in more natural situations and to make more effort. The communication partner may sit increasingly further away from the child so that he or she has to actually approach the adult to initiate the exchange. Next, the picture may be placed at an increasing distance from the child. This means that the child has to go and get it. At this phase, the picture is placed on the front of the child's personal communication book. The picture itself is mounted on card and usually attached by Velcro. There should only be one picture on the front of the book, although other pictures for other preferred items may be kept inside the book. That way they are easily accessible, if there is a need to change the reward. This means that the child has to remove the picture from the communication book to give it to the communication partner. Eventually, the book should be kept in one location at school or at home where the child can easily access it for initiating picture exchanges. It is also important to vary the communication partners so that the child learns to initiate exchanges with different people.

There remains an insistence throughout the PECS programme that the child put the picture right into the communication partner's hand before getting the reward. Bondy and Frost argue that traditional pointing systems present problems with children who have social and communication impairments. Firstly, it can be very difficult at times to tell whether the child has engaged in a communication exchange if he or she is vaguely tapping a picture and, possibly, gazing anywhere but at the communication partner. Indeed, the child may tap more than one picture if not looking.

In contrast, a picture exchange is a distinctive communication act. Secondly, touching a picture will not necessarily engage the attention of somebody who can give the child the desired item. If the child tries to place a picture in a person's hand, it is a very good way of getting attention. There is no need to teach the child to make eye contact with people as a preliminary to a communication exchange. Yet, significantly, touching a picture is nothing like the social act that a picture exchange is. Bondy and Frost suggest that it may be desirable to teach the child to get a person's attention as a preliminary to a communication exchange towards the end of this second phase. They propose that the communication partner should exaggeratedly look away from the child and only look at him or her when actually touched (with physical prompting to establish this if necessary). This way the child comes to learn to hand over the picture only when the attention of the communication partner has been gained.

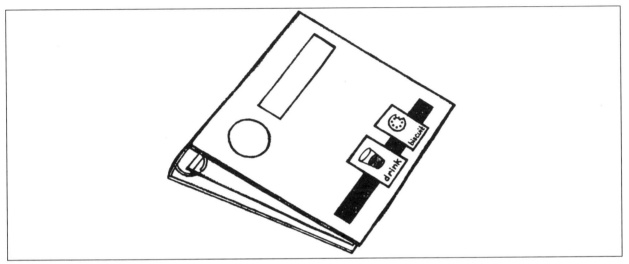

Figure 6.1: shows a communication book which is rather different to those marketed for the PECS approach, but it is used in much the same way. This is an A5 plastic ring binder, easily obtainable from office supplies shops. The dark strip on the front is Velcro to which picture cards adhere because they have a Velcro backing. The white strip is where the child's name is written; the circle is for the child's photo. The binder contains several pages, each with two or three Velcro strips. Other picture cards can be stored inside. In the early stages of teaching there will only be one picture on the front of the book – not two as shown here. The book is hung up on a hook where it is easily accessible.

During the second phase, a variety of additional pictures may be introduced but without making any requirements for discrimination. There is still only one picture and one reward item in view on the communication book at all times. However, the child does learn that a picture exchange can be made to request a range of desired things. The variety of potential rewards that may be used is limited only by the child's particular preferences and interests. At the third phase, the child is taught to discriminate two or more pictures. The communication book now has both the picture for a desired object and a picture of something in which the child has no interest. Bondy and Frost state that it is important that the second picture is not of a preferred item and only the preferred item should be in view. If the picture of the desired thing is given by the child, the adult hands it over. If the child hands over the other picture, the adult says, 'No, we don't have that.' It may be appropriate here to provide a simple gestural prompt to select the correct picture if the child consistently selects the incorrect picture. It is also important to regularly alter the location of the pictures on the book or else the child may learn to select by position rather than according to the picture. This continues until the child is reliably giving the communication partner the correct picture. Then progressively more pictures are added which refer to things that the child is known to like.

Inevitably, some children will have difficulty in learning to discriminate between pictures. There are various strategies that may be worth trying. Pictures could be made larger. Pictures could also be highly coloured with contrasting colours, as in the case of Michael's programme, but it should remain a goal to use the pictures without these extraneous cues. Indeed, if colour is overused, there is a danger that the child will discriminate pictures only by the colour cues rather than by the actual drawings. However, colour cues may be literally faded gradually by using progressively lighter shades of colour over time. Of course, it may be the case that the child does not even notice the picture on the cards and, therefore, it may be worthwhile starting discrimination training with a picture card and a blank card. Object-to-picture matching activities could also be tried. However, Bondy and Frost comment that picture-to-picture matching and picture-to-object matching activities were not helpful with the children with whom they worked because such matching tasks were only weakly rewarding for the children and also they did nothing to promote the development of picture exchanges. A 'last resort' strategy might be to use cards that have both a picture and an object of reference mounted on them. The fact that some items may be edibles need not be a problem: for instance, sweets and the picture for 'sweets' could be covered with laminating film. Depending on the objects used, this strategy may well result in larger cards than cannot easily fit in a conventional communication book and use of such a book would have to be temporarily abandoned. If objects of reference are part of the picture exchange, some way has to be found of fading these. This can sometimes be achieved by a gradual reduction in their size by progressively cutting down the size of the objects. This is most easily done with things like sweet wrappers or crisp bags, but technically it is possible to reduce the size of such things as a ball or a cup until only a tiny bit remains. With some objects, fading must be virtually impossible. Also, with some children, good quality photos may prove to be more successful than symbols.

If all goes well, by this stage the child could be handing over any picture and getting something he or she likes even if it is not the preferred item. Bondy and Frost suggest regular 'correspondence checks' to make sure that the child is actually selecting the picture for the desired thing. They suggest putting two items in view – a preferred item and something that is quite neutral, say, a favoured toy car and a spatula. When the child has given the picture, he or she is allowed to take the appropriate item. If the child gave the picture of the car, the child can have it to play with. However, if the child tries to take the car but gave the picture of the spatula, the teacher would say, 'You asked for the spatula' and point to it. The teacher would then point to the car and say, 'If you want this, then tell me.' Again, some prompting may be necessary.

According to the PECS approach, when a child's communication system contains 12 to 20 pictures, he or she may be taught to build simple sentences. Pictures are arranged in categories, such as toys or activities, either in vertical columns or different pages and may be colour-coded. In this fourth phase, the child is taught to make a request by using the phrase 'I want (the desired thing).' 'I want' is signified by a single picture in the PECS scheme rather than by two separate ones. The child is taught to take the relevant pictures from the communication book and place them on a cardboard strip (the pictures adhere through use of Velcro) and give the entire strip to the communication partner. Initially, the 'I want' picture is already placed on the strip for the child who only has to add the other picture. However, the child is taught through backward chaining to place both pictures in the correct left-to-right sequence on the strip. By the end of this phase the child should have learned to take the picture for the desired item and the 'I want' picture from the communication book. The pictures should always be returned after use to the communication book so that they are ready for use next time. For ease of location, the 'I want' picture should be kept in the same position in the communication book. In this fourth phase, the child is also taught to request things that are not in sight but that are shown to be available. Items that are normally in sight are progressively concealed in cupboards and containers. Of course, situations have to be engineered so that the child is likely to need to request them: for example, an obvious opportunity arises at drinks time if the teacher fails to set out any juice or cups.

In the fifth phase, the child is finally taught to respond to the phrase 'What do you want?' Initially, a preferred object will be placed in the child's view and the teacher will ask the question 'What do you want?' while pointing to the child's 'I want' picture. The child is expected to take the 'I want' picture and the other picture from the book and place it on the sentence strip. Over time, the teacher will introduce a time delay between asking the question and pointing to the card so that the child is increasingly likely to respond before the teacher begins to point to the card and ultimately is responding to the question alone.

In the sixth phase, the child is taught to label or name things in response to specific questions such as 'What do you see?' The child is taught to use a new 'I see' card and the relevant picture card, again taking them from the communication book and placing them on the sentence strip. With many children some form of reward may be necessary to reinforce this labelling and Bondy and Frost recommend that it should not be associated with the pictured thing. Also, they suggest using minimally preferred items. Both strategies are intended to minimise the risks of the child confusing labelling with requesting and becoming upset if he or she does not get the actual item. Beyond this sixth phase, children are taught to use adjectives (e.g. 'I want the big biscuit'), to label own actions and the actions of others, to answer 'yes' and 'no' to specific questions (e.g. 'Do you want this?' or 'Is this a _____?'), and other increasingly complex language.

The overall impression of PECS may be that this is the kind of highly controlled and artificial approach to developing language skills for which behaviourists have often been criticised. The criticism about such approaches is that they can result in robot-like use of simple language forms in very limited settings and that children tend not to use their newly acquired skills spontaneously outside the original teaching settings. However, Bondy and Frost show awareness of these potential problems and at every phase of training recommend that there should be many opportunities to reinforce spontaneous use of acquired skills in a range of settings and with a range of people. Because children with autism in particular can become dependent on visual cues provided by adults to augment their instructions, they place much emphasis upon fading cues as quickly as possible before they do become dependent upon them. Additionally, they are conscious of the need to progressively diminish the use of strong material rewards following every communicative act so that the teaching setting matches more closely the natural daily living settings where children do not typically have their communication attempts reinforced in this manner. These strategies are part of a 'technology of generalisation' which has been established by behaviourists in response to deserved criticisms and which is explained in some detail in the PECS training manual.

In the Delaware programme, PECS has been used with very young children with autism of varying intellectual abilities ranging from children with near normal functioning to children with profound learning difficulties. The majority learned to use two or more pictures in picture exchanges. Many children develop speech during the course of the programme which suggests that communicating with PECS aids general language development. However, many of those who acquire speech continue to need to use pictures as a prop for speaking. Some do not develop speech and have to rely on pictures as their sole means of communication. Bondy and Frost report that PECS has also been used successfully with adolescents and adults with autism and with children with other learning difficulties. There is also some evidence for the success of PECS from reported research in this country by Teresa Webb into using PECS with children with autism and severe learning difficulties. Nevertheless, some important questions remain: for instance, we do not know enough about the children who fail to make progress with PECS; we need to know what strategies best enhance discrimination learning; we do not know whether some types of pictures are easier to use than others (e.g. pictorial representations for things and activities versus geometric symbols for more abstract concepts); and we do not know if some children fare better if they learn to communicate with objects first and if they have opportunities for picture-to-object matching and other matching-to-sample activities. Finally, we need to know what learning and other characteristics mean that children require the somewhat artificial picture exchange approach as a way of breaking down barriers to communication and what skills and knowledge enable children to succeed with more traditional pointing systems based around communication boards and books.

Key summary points
- PECS is described as an example of one approach to teaching the use of picture symbols as an augmentative communication system.
- With children with social and communication impairments the focus should be on teaching them to make a picture exchange in order to obtain high interest items or activities.
- Great care should be taken to avoid children becoming dependent on particular cues for making correct responses.
- Generalisation to other settings and other people must be carefully planned.
- The PECS programme allows for the development of labelling, responding to questions and developing higher order vocabulary at later stages.
- PECS is not the only approach to teaching communication with pictures, and other approaches may be more appropriate for certain groups of children.

References and useful further reading
Baker, S. (1997) *PECS: The Picture Exchange Communication System.* Crawley: West Sussex Educational Psychology and Portage Service.

Bondy, A. & Frost, L. (1994) 'The Picture Exchange Communication System', *Focus on Autistic Behaviour, Vol. 9, No. 3.* Reproduced in Baker (1997).

Webb, T. (2000) 'Can children with autism and severe learning difficulties be taught to communicate spontaneously and effectively using the Picture Exchange Communication System?' *Good Autism Practice,* 3, 29–42.

NB – Computer software for generating a huge range of pictorial symbols is available for machines using Windows from Widgit Software Ltd, 102 Radford Road, Leamington Spa, Warks. CV31 1LF.

Chapter 7: Visual systems for giving information

Visual systems have long been used to support expressive communication by children with learning difficulties. More recently, there have been some useful reports of the use of visual systems to aid receptive communication and this chapter sets out to show some examples. They have been used particularly with children with autism who seem to have difficulties in understanding the language and communication of others when speech is the primary medium used by them. This chapter gives emphasis to some systems that have proved to be useful for children with a range of learning difficulties in both mainstream schools and special schools.

The Division TEACCH (Treatment and Education of Autistic and related Communications handicapped CHildren) is a statewide service for children and adults with autism and communication difficulties in North Carolina. There is not space here to do justice to the philosophy that underpins the TEACCH approach and only some elements are described here. (See their website for an easy introduction: www.teacch.com.) TEACCH aims to provide a supportive environment for these people which circumvents their language and communication difficulties by emphasising the use of visual language rather than spoken language. TEACCH was founded in 1972 under the leadership of Eric Schopler. Together with various colleagues, notably Gary Mesibov, Schopler has developed educational approaches to teaching learning skills, independence and self-control, and communication in a curriculum that has had a significant impact on educational approaches both in the US and in this country. Linda Hodgdon, an American speech and language therapist, has elaborated on visual strategies for communication in a practical resource book for teachers and parents, which describes inventive solutions to a range of communication problems in commonly occurring situations. Hodgdon shows how visual systems of various kinds have been used to give information (e.g. calendars, timetables or menus of activities), to give directions (e.g. classroom rules, recipes, task organisers, worksheets), to organise the environment (e.g. labelling the environment, identifying learning areas and play areas), to celebrate achievements (e.g. in progress files) and to serve as visual bridges between home and school (e.g. through charts which show what the child has done that day).

Use of objects of reference in timetables

As described earlier, Adam Ockelford has produced a book that shows how children with visual impairments might be taught to use a range of objects of reference to express their needs and desires. Ockelford also describes how it may be possible to develop children's anticipation of future events as a next step. Basically, the object of reference is presented by the teacher to the child at the same time as, or followed quickly by, the relevant activity. Initially, the teacher works to make the child associate an object with a current activity, but gradually increases the time between the presentation of the object of reference and the start of the activity. Thus, the child learns that the presentation of an object of reference indicates that an activity is about to begin. The child has to get used to the fact that there may be a delay before the activity starts because it may be the case that the activity has to take place in a totally different part of the school (e.g. dinner in the dining hall, music in a music room).

Once this hurdle has been crossed, it becomes possible to begin to teach the child to anticipate sequences of events by presenting objects of reference in a left-to-right sequence and talking about them: for instance, a ball and a cup placed in a left-to-right sequence could be used to indicate that 'After the ball pool, you can have a drink.' It is critical that this is taught in the context of well-established and frequently occurring routines. Establishing anticipation of a next activity through use of objects of reference is not an easy process but, unless progress can be made at this level, there can be little value in proceeding further with introducing timetables. As regards children and young adults with visual impairments, Ockelford gives examples of the successful use of timetables. For one child, the timetable is made up with a series of boxes with an object of reference in each container. His timetable boxes have lids that can be closed to indicate that an activity is finished which makes it possible to regularly update the timetable and reduce confusion for the child about what comes next. Other approaches to creating timetables described by Keith Park include putting objects of reference in a line on a special shelf or putting them in compartments in a special box or drawer and with each change of activity the object of reference for the completed activity would be removed.

Keith Park notes with some concern that some schools use a separate object of reference to denote each National Curriculum subject. He argues that there is no justification for having these different objects of reference since there cannot be a meaningful distinction between the various subjects for pupils with profound learning difficulties. Surely, categorising teaching activities in terms of subjects can only have relevance for the teacher's planning and assessment records. For many children it is sufficient to establish an object of reference that comes to represent 'sitting down with the others and doing something at the table with the teacher'. A simple gloss would be 'work' for the object of reference when it appears on the timetable. The same object could be used in relation to all work activities if it features in them all as a salient element, e.g. a small bell that is rung at the beginning of every session.

Figure 7.1: shows a sequence of three objects of reference stuck on cards representing a sequence of three activities: a paintbrush to represent 'painting'; a beaker for 'drink'; and a mouse for 'computer'. Each of the three objects has an association with the activity to which it refers for this particular child. Note that a mouse would only make a suitable object of reference for children who actually use one; some children might require a jelly bean switch, for instance. The objects are mounted on laminated card; the objects adhere through the use of Velcro. The cards are hung from hooks on the wall.

Using pictures in visual timetables
The use of pictures in timetables, task organisers and calendars to give information to children with autism and communication disorders is documented better. They have been used with the aim of giving information in a concrete form to help children to cope with the many events during the course of a typical day that can cause confusion or anxiety or frustration. For instance, Hodgdon stresses their value even with children with a good repertoire of language skills, arguing that it is wrong to assume that the routines and activities of a day are known and understood by the children. It may be the case that they recognise and respond appropriately to familiar activities as they occur, but this is not the same as knowing for certain what activities are going to occur and in what sequence. Visual timetables give information in a form that is relatively easy to interpret compared to spoken instructions and they have the potential to clarify what activities are going to occur and the sequence of their occurrence if they are used properly and consistently. Classroom organisation can be substantially improved by the fact that the children know better what activities they are supposed to be doing and where they are going to be done. Individual children who require

support for transitions between activities and changes of location for activities are less likely to forget or be confused or anxious if they have their own timetables to follow. A potential spin-off that is often stressed is that children may become less disruptive of the classroom environment because the use of visual timetables makes them less anxious and less confused and makes it plain that preferred activities will happen alongside the non-preferred ones during each day.

Pictorial symbols representing activities are mounted on a stiff material and displayed on a wall-mounted board. It helps if they are easily removed from the board; they may be stuck on with Blutack; they may be backed with Velcro for use on a cloth-covered board; or they may be backed with magnetic tape for use on a metal board. This kind of arrangement makes it possible to communicate quite clearly that an activity is finished by removing the picture from the timetable. This may be done by the teacher, accompanied by some statement like 'Music is finished now.' Some practitioners recommend getting the children themselves to remove the picture for the completed activity and place it a 'finished' box below the timetable. Certainly, many children seem to enjoy this little routine.

The pictures may be placed in a left-to-right sequence to denote the time sequence of the activities and this is in keeping with the left-to-right movements of reading. However, there is a variety of practice: some workers favour top-to-bottom sequences arguing that they are easier to learn; and some present timetables in a booklet with each activity depicted on a separate page.

It is not possible to show on a visual timetable every single activity during a school day. Indeed, it is most important that the timetables do not become cumbersome and visually cluttered because too many activities are depicted. The timetable can probably only depict the activities for the morning or the afternoon rather than a whole day. Also, the activities that are selected for display must be meaningful for the child. The activities will need names that make sense from the children's point of view and should be noticeably different in terms of teaching materials, settings and/or the people involved. For instance, some activities can have the generic label of 'work', whereas others have specific names such as 'art', 'music' or 'reading'. It is not necessary to have an item for parts of an activity: for instance, 'drinks' as an activity must inevitably entail a routine of fetching the milk or juice, drinks making, tidying and washing up.

Andrew knows that there is going to be swimming today because he has seen his mother put his costume and towel in his school bag. This favourite activity is the highlight of his week at school and as soon as he gets into school he announces 'Swimming, please'. Verbal explanations that he has to wait until after lunch are unlikely to pacify him and there is a serious danger of a temper tantrum occurring with the result that Andrew will miss his swimming. He simply does not have the concept of 'after'. When is 'after lunch'? However, a visual timetable showing the main activities leading up to and following lunch will show him what activities must occur before swimming and that it is truly on the list of planned activities for the day.

So what happens on days when the swimming teacher is absent? Swimming cannot happen, but Andrew does not know this. There is a strong probability that he will have a tantrum when the end of the school day arrives and his favourite activity of the week has not occurred. There are various ways in which the visual timetable can be altered to show this information: for instance, a picture for a replacement activity could be substituted by Andrew's teacher; or the need for a change could be shown by placing a 'NO' sign over the picture for swimming and Andrew could be involved in selecting another liked activity from a selection of possibilities.

In order to understand visual timetables, a child must have awareness that pictures may be used to refer to things or activities. This awareness does not develop of its own accord. Readiness for use of visual timetables may be developed through teaching the children to use pictures for expressive communication and to anticipate a new activity when shown a picture for it. When a child has achieved this basic level of understanding, it may be possible to introduce pictures for two activities – the current activity and next activity only. If this succeeds in getting the child to anticipate what comes next, awareness of longer sequences of activities may be built. Therefore, effective use of class timetables is most likely to occur with children who can understand that a sequence of two or more pictures denotes a sequence of those activities.

The timetables may be on different coloured boards, perhaps personalised further by the addition of a photograph of the child. Pictures need to be 2 inches square at least. The name for the activity should be printed beneath each picture not only for the benefit of supply staff and volunteers, but also because some pupils may begin to learn to recognise the printed words. A child's timetable should be located in a prominent position in order to make it easier for the teacher to show the child when an activity is finished and it is time to move on to the next one. This is crucial to the success of the timetable. A timetable that still shows all of the pictured activities at the end of a morning or afternoon is probably confusing for the child. As soon as one activity is finished, the teacher might say, '(Name for activity) is finished', take the relevant item off the timetable and put it in the 'finished' box. Next, the teacher may say that 'It is now time for (name of next activity)' and point to the relevant picture.

A timetable for the whole class could be useful, although individual pupil timetables are recommended by proponents of TEACCH. Setting up the class timetable for a session could be done with the involvement of the children during a plenary session, for instance, at circle time, at news time, at the beginning or end of the daily mathematics and/or literacy lesson. Thus, the group can discuss what will happen 'first', what happens 'next' and so on. It seems probable that they are more likely to focus in on the timetable and remember the sequence of activities better if they are involved in this way rather than if the teacher has assembled it prior to the session. Also, a focus on the timetable during the plenary at the end of a session may well aid remembering and reflection on the activities by the pupils.

More able children may not need to refer to a wall-mounted timetable. Their timetables could be photocopied sheets which are put in personal organisers containing all the activities for a day, to be checked off as they are done. If they are taken home at the end of the day, these timetables have the added advantage of aiding communication between the children and their parents about what they have done at school that day. Some children may be able to use pictorial calendars for the week.

Most children will have difficulties in following a class timetable for a variety of reasons: for instance, they may not be able to maintain attention on an activity for as long as other children and they may become bored and disruptive; or they may require objects rather than pictures for understanding; they may need more frequent changes of activity to maintain their interest; or short periods of work need to be rewarded by opportunities for short periods of access to preferred activities. Whatever the reason, they need their own individualised timetables which broadly follow the same pattern, but which allow for more individualisation during the available time slots.

In a class of eight Key Stage 1 children, there are individual pupil timetables around the room, each in a permanent location, each a different colour and bearing a picture of the child to whom it belongs. These individual schedules show picture symbols for two or

36

three activities. For one child, there may be access to a computer and this is the first symbol on his or her timetable; for another child, there may be the symbol for 'play' and access to play materials appropriate to the particular session; for another child, there may be a special symbol for one-on-one work in the quiet room; and so on. In each case, the child is prompted to look at his or her timetable, take off the first symbol and go to the designated area where the activity typically takes place. Of course, some children need more guidance and direction than others. After the activity is complete, or the teacher has signalled time for a change around, the children return the first activity symbol to the 'finished box' on their timetables and take the card for the next activity.

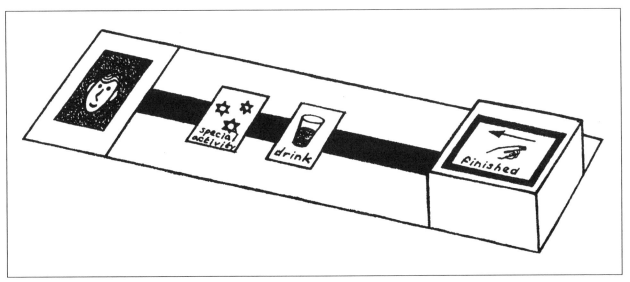

Figure 7.2: shows one pupil's individualised timetable. In order to identify the owner of the timetable, this is put up in its own place in the classroom and bears the pupil's photo. The dark strip is Velcro and the picture cards have Velcro backing. Note the 'finished' box into which cards are put as each activity is completed. One of the cards denotes a special, non-routine activity and this will be followed by drinks time.

Using pictures as task organisers

Pictures can be used in task organisers to help children to perform complete tasks independently. Task organisers consist of a series of pictures showing the sequence of steps required for the completion of an activity. They are most useful for those children who can perform the various steps, but have difficulty with remembering the correct order or who simply get confused. They serve as simple step-by-step prompts for completing a task without the need for constant verbal reminders from an adult. Some children may be able to cope without the task organiser once they have mastered the whole activity. Other children may always be dependent on these tools to keep them focused on the task and to organise themselves, but at least they will not be dependent on an adult. Task organisers can be used for a very wide range of activities: for instance, picture sequences may depict the steps involved in such diverse activities as making a simple meal, accessing a computer, assembling the parts to make a model, using a public pay phone or operating a drinks dispensing machine. Linda Hodgdon offers several examples in her book and examples in a British context are provided by Chris Abbott.

It is not sufficient just to give a child a task organiser: much direction and prompting will be necessary for learning each activity. It is critical to determine the sequence of steps involved in an activity and generate appropriate pictures for each step and associated verbal instructions. In some cases, it may be appropriate to use still photos of the child performing the activities, but often simple pictures will serve. It is also critical to determine whether to teach starting from the first step at the beginning of the sequence or the last step. For each step, the child's attention has to be drawn to the associated picture and the teacher has to state the verbal instruction. With sufficient practice, each picture should serve to trigger recall of the verbal instructions by the child who will then perform the appropriate actions for that step. Of course, the child has to be taught a way of moving correctly through the sequence of pictures and performing each step in turn: for instance, the child may cross off a picture in a photocopied sequence as each step is completed, or a page is turned if the sequence is presented in book form. If necessary, demonstration, physical prompting or gesture should be used by the teacher until the child can perform each step independently and in the correct sequence. At this point it may be possible to begin eliminating the picture cues, but, as noted above, the teacher should not be surprised to find that a child will continue to need access to a visual organiser even when capable of independently performing the various steps.

Key summary points
- Visual timetables may be constructed using objects of reference, picture symbols and photos together with the printed word, as appropriate.
- Timetables may be general class timetables but most pupils require individualised timetables.
- Timetables may be used with pupils who show anticipation when shown a single object or picture to denote a next activity.
- Timetables may show just two activities initially.
- The denoted activities must have relevance and meaning for each child.
- Timetables should be used to show when an activity is finished and what the next activity will be.
- Calendars, diaries and task organisers may be valuable with some children.

References and useful further reading

Abbott, C. (2000) *Symbols Now.* Leamington Spa: Widgit Software.

Hodgdon, L. A. (1995) *Visual Strategies for Improving Communication – Volume 1: Practical Supports for Home and School.* Troy, Michigan: Quirk Roberts Publishing. Available from Winslow Press.

Jackson, E. & Jackson, N. (1999) *Learning Disability in Focus: The Use of Photography in the Care of People with a Learning Disability.* London: Jessica Kingsley.

Watson, L., Lord, C., Schaffer, B. & Schopler, E. (1987) *Teaching Spontaneous Communication to Autistic and Developmentally Handicapped Children.* Austin, Texas: Pro-ed. Available from Winslow Press.

Chapter 8: Reading

The printed word offers pupils the most powerful and flexible visual access system. Next to speech, reading and writing the printed word is the most important mode of communication in our society. The ability to read and write gives us the opportunity to access a huge range of information through a variety of texts which convey skills, knowledge and ideas which could never be learned through direct experience in a lifetime. Just a small personal library of books can give intense pleasure and enjoyment as well as develop our own thinking and insights to a degree which might not be possible through normal interaction with the activities, events, things and people encountered in daily life. Through the use of simple writing tools or sophisticated word processing and email software for personal computers, we can communicate with either intimate friends or immediate family or to a far larger audience, developing our own personal experiences, thoughts, emotions, beliefs, knowledge, ideas and skills. The child or adult who cannot read and write is effectively cut off from many opportunities for communication and personal fulfilment.

Of course, there are people who cannot read for all sorts of reasons; levels of illiteracy are one of the greatest concerns of employers and governments. To a large extent, the handicaps of many people which result from their difficulties with reading and writing can be mitigated by the use of such devices as the television, taped books and the telephone, but they do not provide answers to all of life's problems. This chapter explores the possibilities offered by other forms of graphic representation in providing children and adults with augmentative or alternative systems for reading and writing. Most importantly, it suggests that it is a mistake to identify reading and writing with the printed word alone. The printed word is not the only form of graphic representation that can convey meanings. Indeed, among the earliest known forms of graphic representation used by humans were stylised pictures from which modern forms of the printed word ultimately derive. From this perspective, Braille and Moon systems, for example, can be seen as obvious examples of graphic systems which give access to the world of books and writing for people with severe visual impairments. However, the concept of graphic representation may be extended to include pictures and symbols as well. Therefore, it is possible to argue that children are learning skills that lead to reading when they are learning to, say, discriminate and point to the symbols in a communication book, and it becomes an artificial and unnecessary exercise to try and distinguish such basic acts of communication from reading, which, after all, is only a more sophisticated form of communication.

This inclusive view of reading and writing has implications for many children who have difficulties with reading and writing. Potentially, more widespread use of pictures and symbols in daily living and working environments could open up possibilities for many adults that are currently not available to them. There are a few examples of the use of pictures (for instance, road signs, hazard symbols), but the institutions in our society, including colleges and schools, do not make nearly enough use of them and certainly not in a systematic and planned way. Hopefully, the rest of this chapter will show how much the wider use of such systems of graphic representation could contribute to everybody's lives either as augmentative systems to give wider access to books and information while they are learning to read the printed word or as alternative systems for those people who eventually prove to be incapable of this.

The origin of many of the ideas in this chapter on the use of symbols as augmentative and alternative reading systems may be traced back to a pamphlet by Kathleen Devereux and Judy van Oosterom called *Learning with Rebuses* which was published by the National Council for Special Education in 1984. Sadly, this pamphlet is now out of print, but it contained the distillation of the experiences gained during a decade of language development work at the Rees

Thomas School, Cambridge, by Devereux and van Oosterom with pupils with severe learning difficulties. Rebuses, more commonly (but inaccurately) called symbols, are stylised pictures representing objects, actions and attributes. Although they were not the only people researching the use of symbols, van Oosterom and Devereux can be credited with producing an extensive British glossary of symbols and doing much to establish guiding principles for the use and design of symbols. As Mike and Tina Detheridge explain in their excellent introductory text on using symbols for literacy work, several rather different and much bigger glossaries of symbols, including rebuses, are now in print and are available for symbol processor programmes on computer, which can be likened to ordinary word processing programmes. Although these modern glossaries are vastly extended and improved now, the ancestry of most of them can be traced back to the original symbols contained in the Peabody Rebus Reading Program which Devereux and van Oosterom took as their first source of inspiration for reading, writing and language development work starting in 1974.

Finally, it must be stressed that the benefits of teaching reading for many children with complex learning difficulties may actually go far beyond the acquisition of functional reading skills which aid independence in daily living. Increased proficiency in reading can be a great morale booster for children with learning difficulties and reading can develop into an enjoyable pastime. Sue Buckley and colleagues at the University of Portsmouth have assembled evidence from case studies of teaching reading to children with Down syndrome that there can also be a positive impact on the development of speech and language, auditory perception and memory. The children in these case studies learned to read (with varying degrees of success) and this seemed to result in them producing longer and more grammatical utterances, improved articulation and greater speech intelligibility. Buckley suggests that this is probably because teaching them to read provided frequent opportunities to practise saying sentences which the children could not generate spontaneously even though they understood them. Indeed, she argues that they may learn new vocabulary and grammatical structures more easily from reading than they do from listening to spoken models due to the concrete nature of printed words and their relative difficulties with auditory processing and memory.

Developing concepts
Devereux and van Oosterom describe a variety of language development activities, which serve in many ways as an introduction to reading symbols. The focus of these activities is on the development of vocabulary and the understanding of progressively complex instructions supported through the judicious use of symbols. In practice, they also serve to develop the skills of visual recognition, visual discrimination, visual memory and following left-to-right sequences which underpin reading of the printed word.

One set of games is called 'read, say and do' or 'read, sign and do'. The interest in this activity for many children will be found in its novelty and the opportunities that it presents for them to take turns at being the teacher and controlling others. Symbols may be introduced in PE or movement games in which children are asked to respond to 'Action Cards'. These are A4 size cards depicting the symbol for a verb, such as, 'stand', 'sit', 'walk', 'jump' and 'stop'. The cards are held up in turn by the teacher, who will also say (and sign, as appropriate) the command initially, but who will eventually just hold the cards up silently. When children are able to respond to action cards at this one-word level, they may be taught to respond to more difficult commands involving more grammatical elements (e.g. 'sit on chair', or 'stand on bench') and adjectives and prepositions (e.g. 'throw the big ball', 'stand between the chair and the table'). As a general guide to the order for developing these concepts, van Oosterom and Devereux used the vocabulary suggested by the *Boehm Test of Basic Concepts*, but the *Derbyshire Language Scheme* by Mark Masidlover and Wendy Knowles and the *Living Language Scheme* by Ann

Locke are other sources of ideas about which vocabulary to teach and in what sequence. They also provide clear guides for developing the grammatical complexity of instructions.

At an early stage, children may be taught through a range of game-like activities to match symbols to actual objects and pictures of objects. This is a familiar activity in many classrooms; symbols and pictures or objects are repeatedly associated with one another, for example, by asking children to place objects with their matching symbols or pointing to a symbol and asking the children to find the related object from a display. Devereux and van Oosterom also suggested that pupils should be taught to put together puzzles of symbols in order to focus their attention on the visual characteristics of the symbols. Straight-cut puzzles are recommended, since pupils may respond to the cue of fit alone rather than look at the actual symbols in the case of interlocking jigsaw puzzles. Each puzzle should depict a single symbol and should be cut horizontally or vertically into equal-sized rectangles. Puzzles may be graded in complexity as two-piece, four-piece, six-piece and so on. The actual activity may also be made increasingly complicated by mixing up the pieces from two or more puzzles and cutting puzzles diagonally or into different-sized shapes.

Devereux and van Oosterom also devised a range of 'Listen and Choose' card games. In these games children are shown two or more symbols and asked to find one named by the teacher. A child who chooses correctly gets to keep the card or is given a token and, at the end of the game, the child with the most cards or tokens is the winner. A variation on this game is 'Listen, Look and Point' in which the children are shown a picture or object and have to point to the correct symbol in a display of two or more symbol cards. When children can respond to pictures of single objects or actions, the level of complexity can be increased by introducing pictures that show people or animals doing particular actions (e.g. 'boy sitting', 'boy standing', 'dog sitting' and 'dog standing') or having particular attributes (e.g. 'red car' and 'blue car') or in particular places (e.g. 'cat on chair' and 'cat under chair'). At these later levels, the children choose which one of two or more 'symbol sentences' (i.e. cards showing the symbols for the actor and action, attribute and actor, etc. in an appropriate left-to-right sequence) relates to a particular picture, or vice versa.

Lotto games may be used to teach matching of pictures to symbols and symbols to symbols. At a basic level, Devereux and van Oosterom introduced a board for each player with four objects or actions. The boards may differ only in location of the pictures or symbols or in the ones that are shown. This may be a simple 'bingo' game where the pupils match the picture or symbol flash cards which are displayed by a dealer to the associated symbol on the baseboard. The first person to complete his or her baseboard is the winner.

At later levels of complexity, the children may be required to attend to two or more features of the pictures in that they may show, say, an object with a particular attribute (e.g. 'big dog', etc.) or an agent performing an action (e.g. 'fish swimming', etc.). Correspondingly, the square on the base boards and the symbol flash cards show two or more related symbols. The children must notice two features in the pictures or symbols on the boards to be sure of making a correct response.

Devereux and van Oosterom describe how simple posting boxes may be used to help build up recognition and discriminatory skills. In these, two or more posting boxes and a selection of symbol flash cards are used and the children have to sort and post cards in the appropriate box. The games may be simple symbol-symbol matching games in that symbol cards have to be posted in the box bearing the symbol. Similarly, classification skills may be developed by posting cards according to the category of the objects (e.g. all the toys in the box marked 'toys', all the animals in the box marked 'animals'). The children may even check for themselves that the correct cards had been posted in a box by the simple expedient of putting a particular colour dab on the back of each card.

A variety of race board games may be developed as a vehicle for reinforcing recognition and discrimination. For instance, Devereux and van Oosterom describe 'First Home' which comprises a die with colour spots on its faces and a board with a number of corresponding colour dabs. If the child throws a red, his or her piece may move to the next red square. Equally, the die and the board could have symbols for objects or actions.

Devereux and van Oosterom also used the school's stock of miniature figures and people (e.g. Playmobil people, Britain's farm people and animals) in a range of graded activities for developing concepts. For instance, one set of materials included a farmyard set with plastic animals, trees, fences, gates and a pond. A series of symbol sentences of graded complexity were developed for the set using a grammar scope and sequence developed by David Crystal. People doing the same activity today could just as easily use the *Derbyshire Language Scheme* or the syntax programme in *Living Language* as a guide for activities and selecting structures for teaching. In the farmyard game, the children may either be shown a symbol sentence and move the relevant pieces around the farm board (e.g. they put the cow in the pond when shown 'cow in pond') or the teacher may put a toy in a particular place and encourage the children to find the appropriate symbol sentence in a display or indeed construct one using available cards.

Devereux and van Oosterom also developed a series of activities with worksheets for independent learning activities; the first step was ringing (i.e. 'draw a ring round the X'), the next was colouring (i.e. 'colour the X'), the third was drawing (i.e. 'draw an X'), the fourth was copying (i.e. 'copy the X') and the last was writing (i.e. 'write X'). All instructions started with the single symbol (NB – 'draw a ring round' is a single symbol denoting 'encircle'), as in 'draw a circle' or 'put a ring round the baby'. The symbol instructions were introduced in a variety of practical activities related to English or mathematics, such as drawing a circle around all of the pictures of horses on a sheet stamped with various animals. Worksheets covered with acetate were introduced carefully and the children were given chinagraph pencils or felt tip pens to write on these. These worksheets consisted of pictures with the accompanying symbol instructions and were used to reinforce learning of concepts and language being taught in other activities. Children's work cards might also instruct them to draw or write particular things in their exercise books (e.g. 'draw a house', 'colour the door red', 'write book', etc.)

Key summary points
- Literacy is a form of communication.
- The visual medium for reading and writing need not just be the written word, but can also include pictures and symbols.
- Literacy can have a powerful impact on personal self-esteem, independence, concept development and language development.
- Symbols can be introduced through a range of games.

Reading books
Obviously, following from the inclusive view of reading proposed above, the activities described by Devereux and van Oosterom are just as much reading activities as language development activities. They should not be regarded as 'pre-reading activities', but they do demonstrate how symbols may be used for memory and language development activities long before an ability to read the printed word is established. However, now it is necessary to explore here how reading might be taught to children with complex learning difficulties.

Children have to be convinced that written language can meet their personal and social needs if they are going to be motivated to learn to read and practise their reading skills. Therefore, it is most important to develop children's interest in books and show that they can be relevant to their world and provide useful information besides being enjoyable. This can be done at an early stage even with children who have very severe learning difficulties. The MENCAP organisation has produced a pack for teachers and parents of pupils with severe and profound learning difficulties which illustrates well how a range of books may be shared with children who are developmentally quite young and cannot read. The pack contains a series of examples of how books and plays have been adapted for story telling using tactile books as well as ordinary books, and systematically relating actual objects and activities to aspects of the texts by, for instance, providing interesting tactile sensations of items, using musical instruments to make particular sounds, giving opportunities to taste and smell things, and organising movement activities.

Rumble in the Jungle is a delightful book containing colourful pictures of a variety of animals – monkey, tiger, elephant, lion and so on. The resources needed for telling the story can be teacher-made or the children can be involved in producing them in some of the activities associated with the book. Animal masks and toy models of animals are useful props – so too are noise makers, leaves and different textures of materials. Not all of the text of the book has to be used because that could make the story telling too long and complicated. Also, the children should be involved in feeling the textures associated with the animal's fur and hair, making animal noises, wearing animal masks and the like. So on the page where the author has written 'It's great to be a chimpanzee swinging in the trees', the teacher or a child wears the monkey mask and moves around from child to child in the group making monkey sounds. Alternatively, a toy monkey could be passed around for each child to feel as the teacher repeats the line. Children might be encouraged to sign 'monkey' as the word is said or to feel the fur of the toy. The session is lively and enjoyable and introduces interesting sounds, sights and textures to supplement those on the pages in the book. The aim of repeated readings is for the children to begin to anticipate words or particular experiences at key points in the story telling.

These multi-sensory approaches combined with frequent repetition of telling the stories and careful modification of the language used, get around the problem that all books, even the best picture books, are based in language which children with learning difficulties may not comprehend. This approach to introducing literature to children with severe and profound and multiple learning difficulties has been developed considerably by Keith Park and Nicola Grove. However, no matter how relevant, valuable and creative these approaches may be, the focus here is upon how pictures and symbols may be used to develop children's ability to read texts with a degree of independence and enjoyment.

Alongside these developments, structured reading programmes can be implemented. Most work with children with complex learning difficulties emphasises the use of so-called 'look and say' methods, initially. Typically, the first phase of teaching reading involves establishing a small sight vocabulary, choosing words and sentences used in everyday speech, and encouraging building of phrases and sentences with this sight vocabulary. Subsequent work will involve continuing to expand this sight vocabulary, but will also teach grapheme-phoneme (letter-sound) correspondences using words children can already read in order to develop word attack skills for new words encountered in print. Phonics approaches that emphasise teaching grapheme-phoneme correspondences from the outset are seldom used, due to widely held beliefs about the children's likely language and memory difficulties. However, in many respects, phonological awareness can be developed using methods incorporating visual cues, as long as there remains an insistence on accurate assessment of each child's vocabulary knowledge and auditory processing ability. The approach to identifying phonemes in speech and writing, the blending of phonemes for reading and the process of segmenting words into phonemes for spelling, as described in the INSET materials for the National Literacy Strategy, can be supported visually. For example, it is helpful when words with common letter strings are written and displayed for children in 'word families' and simple devices such as phonic wheels can be very useful visual aids.

Sue Buckley's work was based on the reasonable analysis that there are three general strategies adopted by readers when trying to read novel sentences of text: a visual strategy involves somehow comparing the words encountered in the text with visual images stored in memory and, hopefully, recognising them as known words; a phonological strategy, developed through learning grapheme-phoneme rules, enables children to 'sound out' unfamiliar words and find a matching auditory trace of the spoken word in memory; and a context strategy enables the printed word to be guessed by working out which word will fit grammatically and semantically in a sentence. Of course, all three strategies may be used simultaneously in reading, but Buckley found that children with Down syndrome tend to be visual readers. This is because they often lack the knowledge of vocabulary and grammar for using the phonological and context strategies: a word can only be recognised through sounding out if it is actually in the child's vocabulary; a word can only be guessed from its context if it is a word that the child knows and the rest of the sentence is properly understood; and children may not be able to hear all the sounds in words due to hearing loss and auditory processing problems. Typically, this held to be true of many other children with complex learning difficulties besides children with Down syndrome. In extreme cases, children may read words and sentences quite well using visual strategy but have no understanding of what the word or the whole sentence means, i.e. they are 'barking at print'. Therefore, it is very important that teachers know each individual child's level of language development and introduce words and sentences in print that are mostly in his or her grasp. However, since children can acquire new language and memory skills from reading, a fine balance has to be struck between introducing some new vocabulary and structures in text while keeping the majority of text at a level where the child's understanding is optimal.

The teaching strategies used with children with learning difficulties may be essentially the same as those used with all children, even though teachers do need to take into account their relative delays in the development of language skills and memory function. The first consideration is how to teach children about the basic conventions of reading (e.g. start at the front of the book, turn over the pages one at a time, start at the top of the page and read from left to right) and to establish the notion that printed words are spoken words written down. The only truly interesting and meaningful way of introducing books and teaching these concepts is to read to or with children and to make the whole activity pleasurable. In order to be effective with children with complex learning difficulties, it will have to be done regularly and may have to be done with individuals or small groups (matched carefully according to ability) rather than with the whole class as in the shared reading activity prescribed in the National Literacy Strategy. Also, in the case of children with auditory processing difficulties, the phonics work required by the National Literacy Strategy may not proceed as rapidly with these children as it may with average learners and, indeed, many activities will focus on the systematic development of auditory memory and discrimination skills for a considerable length of time before any sound-letter associations may be taught. Strategies for teaching reading will make use of other methods recommended in the National Literacy Strategy guidance, such as reading aloud to the children varying tone and expression but at a measured pace, pointing to each word while following the lines of print. Books with clear but interesting illustrations and print of a good size should be used. The children may be involved in reading at the level that is appropriate to them: the teacher may ask them to read along with him or her, either by talking or by signing or both together; the teacher may encourage them to point to particular details in the pictures; the children may be encouraged to make predictions and comments and to ask questions.

'Predictable books' are excellent books to read with younger children who are at the beginning stages of learning to read. They are called predictable because they have the following characteristics:

- The stories are well known and familiar ones such as 'Goldilocks and the Three Bears'. On the whole children learn to read best stories that are well liked and well known. They are more likely to spontaneously predict or anticipate what will happen next because they feel that they can do so without fear of being wrong. Almost inevitably, they will join in the telling of the story or can more easily be induced to do so. If the story is well told, repetition helps learning.
- These stories have a repetitive pattern that can be found throughout. For instance, in the Goldilocks story you have the three bears each asking in turn, 'Who's been eating my porridge?', 'Who's been sitting in my chair?' etc. Therefore, there is a special refrain that the children can predict and they can join with the teacher in the reading.
- Some stories have a cumulative pattern. For instance, in 'The Great Big Enormous Turnip' by Tolstoy, several characters in turn become involved in helping an old man pull up a huge turnip until finally:

> The mouse pulled the cat,
> The cat pulled the dog,
> The dog pulled the granddaughter,
> The granddaughter pulled the old woman,
> The old woman pulled the old man,
> The old man pulled the turnip.

At this early stage of reading, the children may not accurately recognise words. Some may well be relying on memory when they 'read' words or whole sections of familiar books. Nevertheless, they are learning skills of prediction and are developing concepts about print that are crucial to subsequent development of reading skills.

Teachers have a vast range of children's literature from which to choose appropriate books, including a number of well-designed but costly reading development schemes. However, a problem with reading schemes is that they are designed for the average learner and often proceed at too fast a pace in terms of the vocabulary and language structures used and the expectations of knowledge of phonics and ability to learn to recognise new words quickly. That is why 'language-experience' approaches have long been favoured for use with young children and children with learning difficulties. Language-experience approaches are based on the assumption that no commercially produced book can be as meaningful to a child as a story based upon his or her own immediate experience. This does not mean that books published for children have no appeal or educational value, but these should be chosen carefully to suit the individual child and should not wholly replace 'made-up' stories.

Language experience methods can help beginning readers to realise that written language is mostly just ordinary talk written down. Another major advantage of language-experience approaches is that they bring together the reading and writing of written language in a unified programme. With average learners, a typical sequence of steps in producing a story might be as follows:

Step 1: The child should be encouraged to tell a story based upon his or her experience.
Step 2: The teacher writes down the story while the child is dictating it.
Step 3: The child is asked subsequently to read the story aloud.
Step 4: The teacher points out and teaches recognition of key words.

The basic approach is relevant to most children with learning difficulties. Key elements which should feature include:

- Creation of simple personal books or interest books. Photos are chosen by the children, perhaps of a recent trip or event, or alternatively pictures cut from magazines and stuck in their own individual book. Beneath each picture the teacher writes the word. For each word there should be a matching card with the word printed on it, since this makes possible a range of activities aimed at teaching association of words with the pictured objects, actions etc. These books can be sent home for practice with parents or may ultimately be used as 'dictionaries' for reference and helping with written work.
- A range of simple games which are fun for the children and help provide the necessary repetition. For instance, lotto, bingo and snap can be played for enjoyment using word cards.
- Labelling objects in classrooms and school as a reinforcement activity. Word cards are stuck to various items throughout the school. The children can be encouraged to play games of matching word cards to those stuck on the items. Labelling may be done with simple phrases rather than just single words, e.g. 'here is the door', 'this is a window', etc. This helps to introduce the 'basic words' which are repeated so often in texts and which cannot be depicted.
- Diaries or news books can be made up. These are essentially similar to the interest books. The child draws a picture of whatever he or she wishes and dictates a caption to the teacher who writes it down.
- Children who know a number of words may be introduced to sentence making. The *Breakthrough to Literacy* scheme developed project folders in which each child may keep known words and may use these to create and copy out sentences. The sentences can simply be displayed on sentence holders if the child is not able to write well. The children can be encouraged to produce sentences to describe details in a picture, answer questions about a story, to describe an action demonstrated by the teacher and so on.

Wordless picture books use pictures alone to tell a story or sequence of events. Words are not necessary, so children can 'read' the books by themselves. However, these books are used to the greatest advantage when a teacher shares them with the children and encourages them to talk about the story content. There are a large number of picture books that have attractive illustrations, have interesting topics and provide stimulating activities for language development. The books often have enough visual appeal to stimulate many children to tell the story and to make inferences and predictions. Language development techniques of modelling, expansion and/or extension may be used to guide the children to produce richer and more sophisticated utterances for telling the stories in terms of vocabulary and grammatical structures. At a later stage, the children's own sentences may be written down as part of teaching word recognition.

Key summary points
- Reading books to and with children should be an enjoyable activity.
- The activity can be made more meaningful by modifying the author's language and by introducing props and activities to make reading a multi-sensory experience.
- Children should be encouraged to anticipate words and events at key points in the story.
- The first phase of teaching actual reading should emphasis developing a sight vocabulary.

- Phonics teaching tends to come later due to auditory processing and auditory memory difficulties of children.
- Teaching strategies are essentially those used with all children.
- There should be a greater emphasis upon language-experience approaches with children with learning difficulties with simple games, interest books, diary/news books and sentence making with word cards.
- Predictable books and wordless picture books can be valuable resources but any books with good pictures can be modified to suit individual needs.

Using symbols as a bridge to teaching word recognition

These approaches to teaching reading emphasise the need to develop quickly the association between spoken and written language. A key question is whether this process can be facilitated through use of signs and symbols. The response seems to be in the affirmative, although the evidence is largely found in anecdotal case studies. These show that symbol reading activities can be developed as part of an augmentative system to be used while developing an ability to read the printed word. Since most symbols are essentially stylised pictures, symbols are easier to learn and to remember than printed words. Therefore, children are enabled to devote their attention to the meaning of a phrase, sentence or story rather than to identification of words and do not develop an antipathy to books through repeated failure. However, an ability to read printed words will not necessarily develop by a process of osmosis, although there is anecdotal evidence of children learning incidentally to recognise printed words. In an augmentative reading system, symbols should have the actual word printed beneath them and, as soon as possible, the symbols must be faded out and be replaced by the printed word. Inevitably, many pupils with complex learning difficulties will remain wholly dependent on an alternative system whereby the same symbols help them to, say, follow simple instructions, compose shopping lists and other lists, keep diaries or schedules and so on.

In order to match activities to the interests and experiences of the children, the emphasis may be on teaching children to read single symbols and sentences made up of short series of symbols using the language-experience approaches described above. The language-experience approach demands that teachers start from a solid base of knowledge about each individual child's comprehension of vocabulary and grammar and ability to recognise pictures and symbols. If the aim in these activities is to teach reading skills rather than develop language, it is most important that pupils are taught to recognise symbols only for those words that they already know and to read symbol sequences that relate to sentence structures that they already comprehend.

The modification to the language-experience approach requires very little equipment: flash cards with symbols for chosen words; flash cards for particular people or places may be represented by actual photos or stylised drawings; flash cards for colours show irregularly shaped patches of colour; a range of interesting pictures; a simple holder to prop up sequences of symbol cards. It helps if the teacher is able to draw recognisable symbols for the children: they do not have to look like the work of a professional artist and, in fact, the symbols in some of the commercially published glossaries have been created so that they may be easily drawn. Some flash cards should show the symbol with the word printed underneath in bold, lower case letters; other cards should show the word alone, although it is useful for some games to have the symbol on the reverse. For the less confident person, Mike and Tina Detheridge describe a range of supportive software for computers from their own firm, Widgit Software, and others that enables teachers to print out symbols and the associated words using huge glossaries of symbols. The teaching skill lies in the assessments, selection of objectives, process of task analysis, selection of teaching material and the ways of motivating and involving the children. The actual teaching methods are simple variants on standard look-and-say methods for teaching reading.

A variant of the 'sentence reading method' focuses on teaching word recognition in the context of reading symbol sentences into which some printed words are carefully introduced when the children are ready:

- The teacher selects some cards which can be combined to make a simple sentence and talks about the symbols with the children. It helps to have actual items or a picture of them that the sentence represents, e.g. a picture of John wearing a hat to go with the symbol sentence 'John has a red hat.'
- The teacher puts the cards on the table in appropriate order, saying the sentence slowly and clearly and pointing to the relevant card while saying the word.
- The teacher encourages the children to say and/or sign each word as the cards are pointed to, giving verbal prompts as necessary. When the children can do this easily, the teacher should increase the speed of pointing so that the string of words is said/signed quicker by the children and sounds more like a sentence.
- The teacher chooses another picture and related symbol sentence and teaches in the same way. Revision of learned sentences briefly at the end of each session is beneficial.
- Thus far, the method is no different from the approach to encourage development of spoken language. However, when the children can recognise and name/sign about a dozen symbols in sentences, the teacher should clearly print the words on one or two of the symbol cards below the symbols. Reading continues in the same way as before but the teacher emphasises the printed word on coming to those cards.
- The symbols are eliminated for those key flash cards, when it seems that the children are aware of the one or two printed words in the sentence. Thus, the sentence is made up of one or two word cards and symbol cards.
- The teacher continues until all symbols are eliminated and the children are reading sentences of printed words only. The children can be encouraged to rearrange the cards to create their own sentences.

Another approach is the 'single word recognition method': children are taught to read a number of individual symbols and then the words. The approach may complement the sentence reading method because children may be taught to put learned words together in simple sentences.

- The teacher shows two or three symbol/word cards to the children and talks about them. The printed word is pointed out and the children are told, 'This says (name).' They are encouraged to say/sign the word with the teacher.
- The teacher fades out any prompts until the children are able to say the words correctly when the teacher points to the symbol/word cards.
- The aim here is to play a matching game. The children are shown the word cards and are encouraged to find the matching symbol/word card. In this context, the teacher may find it helpful to point out any distinguishing features of the words (e.g. tails to letters, long word, round letters, etc.) The teacher continues to ask the children to say/sign the words. Supplementary activities might be lotto, bingo, snap and dominoes games which emphasise word-word matching.
- When the children can match word cards to symbol/word cards, the teacher works at getting them to read the word cards only. The activity can be supplemented by little games, such as pinning words to a notice board and asking the children to find a particular one. The words could be kept in a special wallet or box and the children allowed to open it and look at the words frequently.
- The sequence is then repeated with another set of two or three words, but revision time is allowed for recognition of the original set of words.
- When the children can read about 12 to 20 words, they can be taught to read simple sentences made up by the teacher using these words or to make up their own sentences.

Felicity Fletcher-Campbell has produced an extensive review of the literature on teaching literacy to children with learning difficulties. There has been little research on developing effective teaching techniques with children with complex learning difficulties, but it is easy to adapt the above methods and experiment systematically to find out what works best with each individual child. For many children with learning difficulties, it may be necessary to develop a range of fun and meaningful activities which permit regular revision and practice of the same few words without boring the child (e.g. treasure hunts for words, fishing games, word lotto, word dominoes and word bingo). It is possible to introduce painting words and letters, using magnetic letters, making words out of dough or clay and baking them, modelling them in plasticene, etc. Also, it is essential to ensure that the children recognise the words learned in new contexts (e.g. in new books or magazines or on signs in the community) and that they recognise them when the size and shapes of the letters are somewhat different.

Fading the symbols is often easier said than done because children can become over-dependent on the visual cue. Devereux and van Oosterom comment that there is some research evidence that use of 'integrated picture cues' may be useful as an intermediate stage between using symbols and using printed words. This method embeds symbols into the actual words so that, presumably, the reader's eye is led along the line of print and he or she may note some of the visual characteristics of the words themselves. The embedded symbols may actually replace a letter (e.g. the symbol 'ball' may replace the letter 'a' in the word 'ball') or be integrated into a letter, perhaps by printing it in another colour to reduce visual clutter.

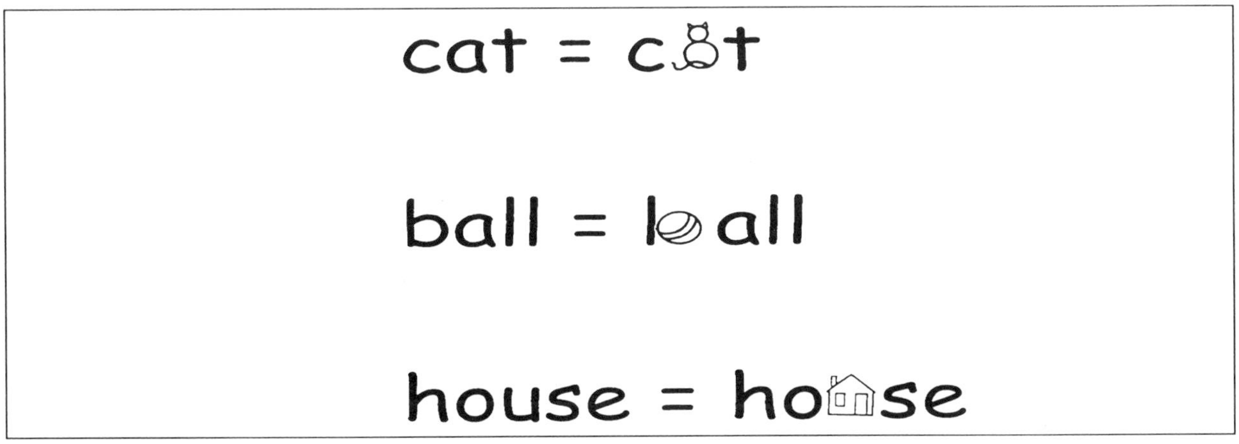

Figure 8.1: There is some evidence that an integrated picture cue may help some children to focus on the shape of the printed word and to learn to recognise it. In the word 'ball' the picture symbol is integrated into the letter 'b'. In the other two words, the picture symbol actually replaces a letter. The value of this approach has yet to be demonstrated unequivocally and teachers may encounter problems in fading the visual cues. Nevertheless, it may be worthwhile experimenting with the approach. Possibly, much depends upon retaining the letters that form the characteristic pattern or shape of the word.

A second question to be answered is whether, in the case of children with good comprehension but poor expressive skills, teaching may proceed in a purely receptive mode. This approach is needed for working with those children who cannot speak or sign for physical reasons. In theory, the teaching activities described above might be modified so that they may proceed purely in the receptive mode. However, in order to check that a child is learning to read, the teacher has to devise some simple checks of comprehension since the child cannot speak or sign. For instance, the teacher might arrange sequences of flash cards either to form instructions for the children to do certain things or to require the children to indicate a particular picture from a display which is associated with a particular sentence.

Key summary points
- The association between written and spoken language may be facilitated by the use of signs and symbols.
- Standard sentence reading and word recognition methods require some modification to incorporate signs and symbols.
- Fading symbols and signs requires careful planning.
- Embedded symbols may be helpful.

Using information and communication technology

Children can have access to books by the simple expedient of inserting new lines of text into them which either incorporate symbols for key words plus some printed words or consist wholly of symbol sequences. A major change in teaching methods has been brought about by the development of a range of symbol processing software. The books by Chris Abbot and by Tina and Mike Detheridge are valuable resources for teachers containing descriptions of the ways in which various software suites may be used by teachers, to improve literacy skills through use of symbols. They also provide details about key technological innovations (e.g. on-screen grids, concept keyboards) which have made computers and communication devices accessible to pupils with a range of disabilities. These innovations have made it possible for teachers to generate a huge range of reading material for children using both printed words and symbols together: they can easily produce modified text for informational and story books to make them more accessible; they can produce scripts for plays; they can write instructions for children to follow; they can provide captions for displays; and so on. With appropriate support many children can produce their own material: they can produce captions for their pictures; they can write their own stories; they can write letters to people in distant places; they can use email; they can produce symbol newspapers; they can write poems; and so on. The advent of digital cameras and cheap scanners has made it possible to record a range of activities and events as they occur and to produce indelible records of experience which might otherwise fade quickly from memory. Expansions of the various standard glossaries have made it possible to have symbols for vocabulary related to each subject area of the curriculum: for instance, there are symbols for history artefacts; symbols for use on weather charts, maps and worksheets for field trips in geography; religious symbols and symbols for emotions and feelings for spiritual development; symbols for health education and sex education programmes; symbols for use in food technology projects; and symbols for use in pupils' evaluations of activities and records of achievement.

One of the advantages of using symbol processing software is that the process of producing text with associated symbols is so much easier. However, when using symbols (and signs), people must think clearly about the language that they use with children. It is usually the case that existing text cannot be typed into a simple word processor without careful modification because the resulting strings of symbols may be just as confusing: for instance, the code of behaviour that states 'help other people' might make more sense if rewritten as 'help people' since 'other' is not a simple concept and the symbol offers no clarification. Also, the degree of symbolisation for text needs some careful consideration: on the one hand, symbolising all words may well be the best way of supporting a language-experience approach to reading printed words; on the other hand, use of key words only may get the message across satisfactorily and reduce visual clutter in informational displays, codes of conduct, comprehension worksheets, instruction cards and the like.

Fletcher-Campbell notes that some commentators are more cautious about the role of information and communication technology in promoting literacy skills. There are calls for a more thorough examination of the pedagogical issues raised by its use. Also, many teachers are still struggling to come to grips with the rapidly changing technologies. Finally, when all is said and done, information and communication technology is just another tool and teachers have to take care that its use observes the principles that underpin best teaching practice.

Key summary points
- There are positive reasons for enthusing about the potential contribution of information and communications technology to literacy learning.
- New technologies require careful evaluation and use by teachers who understand fully both the technologies and the principles underpinning best practice in teaching literacy.

References and useful further reading
Abbot, C. (2001) *Symbols Now.* Leamington Spa: Widgit Software.

Andreae, G. (1998) *Rumble in the Jungle.* London: Orchard Books.

Boehm, A. E. (2000) *Boehm Test of Basic Concepts* 3rd Edition (Boehm-3) The Psychological Corporation.

Buckley, S. & others (1993) *The Development of Language and Reading Skills in Children with Down's Syndrome.* Portsmouth: University of Portsmouth.

Crystal, D., Fletcher, P. & Garman, M. (1976) *The Grammatical Analysis of Language Disability: A Procedure for Assessment and Remediation.* London: Edward Arnold.

Detheridge, T. & Detheridge, M. (1997) *Literacy through Symbols: Improving Access for Children and Adults.* London: David Fulton Publishers.

Devereux, K. & van Oosterom, J. (1984*) Learning with Rebuses.* Stratford-upon-Avon: National Council for Special Education.

Fletcher-Cambell, F. (2000) (Ed.) *Literacy and Special Educational Needs: A Review of the Literature.* Research Report 227. London: DfEE.

Grove, N. (1998) *Literature for All: Developing Literature in the Curriculum for Pupils with Special Educational Needs.* London: David Fulton Publishers.

Lawton, J. S. (Ed.) & others (1999) *Reading for All: Ideas for Story Telling for Children and Young Adults with Severe and Profound Learning Disabilities.* London: MENCAP.

Locke, A. (1995) *Living Language.* Windsor: NFER-Nelson.

Masidlover, M. & Knowles, W. (1980) *Derbyshire Language Scheme.* Private Publication: Ripley, Derbyshire.

Park, K. (1998) 'Dickens for all: inclusive approaches to literature and communication for people with severe and profound learning disabilities', *British Journal of Special Education,* 25, 3, 114–18.

The Breakthrough to Literacy Scheme is published by Longman (www.longman.co.uk).

Walker, M. (ed) (1996) *Symbols for Makaton.* Revised version. Camberley: Makaton Vocabulary Development Project.

Chapter 9: Developing mathematical understanding

Not so long ago, mathematics was perceived as largely irrelevant to the lives of many children with complex needs, especially those who had severe or profound learning difficulties. Staff were often concerned that at best children would be learning skills of counting and computation without the necessary understanding to use them confidently in daily life. Research carried out in the 1960s and 1970s largely supported this conclusion as children's difficulties or deficits were highlighted. Children were described as learning rote skills. In fact, a closer examination of the evidence would have revealed that, as with mainstream pupils, there is large individual variation. Moreover, it is likely that the methods being used did not support the development of understanding, with children being moved as quickly as possible to paper and pencil exercises.

The introduction of the National Curriculum has led teachers to reconsider the place of mathematics and this has been furthered by the introduction of the National Numeracy Strategy with an expectation of a daily lesson in mathematics for pupils from reception through now to Key Stage 3. While the strategy puts heavy emphasis on developing mental maths, there has been attention to the needs of pupils with SEN and a widening of the debate about the role of mathematics. In the National Curriculum handbook there is a reminder that 'Mathematics equips pupils with a uniquely powerful set of tools to understand and to change the world.' Some authors of books on mathematics for pupils with special educational needs have stressed the underlying importance in mathematics of relationships and more specifically of being able to anticipate, predict and problem solve. We need to consider what this means for pupils with complex learning needs.

Consider the following scenario:

Daniel is with his father in a fast food restaurant. His father is buying burgers and chips – Daniel's favourite food. His father orders one cheeseburger (for Daniel) and a special spiceyburger for himself, together with two portions of fries, a coke and a coffee. Daniel watches the food being assembled. Onto the tray go two burger boxes, a cup of coffee and a beaker of coke, and one bag of chips. Immediately he notices that some chips are missing and points to the machine. The second bag quickly arrives. When they get to the table he helps his father unload the tray, one burger for his father and one for him, one bag of chips for his father and one for him...

Daniel has very limited language and no spoken speech. He is not able to count. However, this situation does not require counting skills. It provides a situation in which the pupil is interested and attentive, keen to see what is going on. The outcome of the activity is highly important for him.

David Banes, writing about the curriculum for pupils with physical and additional learning difficulties, provides the following definitions:

'Mathematics is important to all pupils, it provides a means of viewing and making sense of the world and appreciating the relationships between parts of the world and structures those parts create... Mathematics has the capacity not only to describe but also to predict and explain. For pupils of all abilities, therefore, mathematical skills are essential in the development of independence and decision making as pupils begin to understand the world in which they live.'

(Banes, 1999, p.73)

Recognising the importance of number

Research by the first author with pupils with severe learning difficulties and with nursery children highlighted how interested in number children often are. Children in both school and nursery settings, for example, often chose activities which involved number – selecting particular computer activities, floor games and table top activities. They also introduced number into conversation, with talk around birthday parties and ages, around football matches and goals. Staff, in contrast, often seemed reticent to use number words with the children – for example they talked about 'one, and another one and another one', rather than saying 'two' or 'three'. It was almost as if they screened out these words as too difficult for the pupils since they often used them in conversations with other adults in the room. In fact, number words appear quite early in the vocabulary of typically developing children, before the first colour words. This may be unsurprising if we consider that the outcome of decisions about number can be very important for the child. It is also a stable concept – two is always two, and three is always three. Colour on the other hand is a relative term. Red is sometimes maroon, orange or even pink, and in the dark may appear brown.

As we shall see, although a perceptual understanding appears to develop quite early, learners need to be exposed to a number-rich environment if they are to be encouraged to build on this awareness to develop useful problem-solving skills.

Early perceptual development

Number as a perceptual skill also appears to be acquired early. Indeed, some researchers have even stated that it is innate. Babies of five months and younger have been found to be able to discriminate between two arrays on the basis of differences in number – usually when the display contains one, two or three items. This ability is not limited to visual patterns as babies have similarly been found to discriminate between beats of two and three. They have also been able to discriminate between the physical actions of a puppet who jumps either two or three times. In a series of ingenious studies using a puppet and a screen, young infants have been found to be able to predict the outcome of adding and subtracting one, to one and two puppets. Infants have seen the entrance of one puppet, the screen has gone up to obscure this puppet and they have then seen a second puppet join him. When the screen goes back and there is only one puppet rather than the expected two, they show surprise. This result is carefully monitored by an independent observer who does not know whether the baby is looking at a correct or incorrect display.

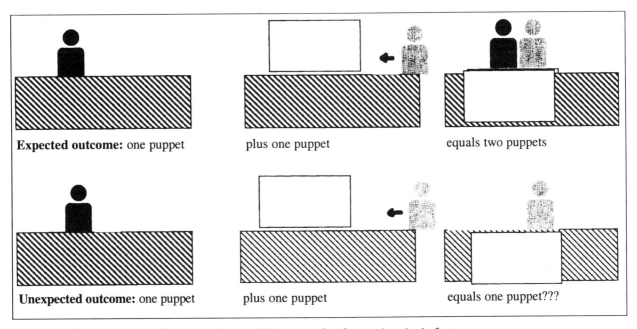

Expected outcome: one puppet   plus one puppet   equals two puppets

Unexpected outcome: one puppet   plus one puppet   equals one puppet???

Figure 9.1: Apparatus for assessing addition and subtraction in infants.

This early cognitive skill can be seen as an extension of object permanence, demonstrating understanding that, not only does an object exist when you can not see it, but if there are two items, they will still be two even if they are hidden from view. Activities that teachers develop to promote this awareness could be developed to include a number dimension. One is reminded of the rhyme 'Two little dicky birds sitting on a wall', a rhyme that has a lot to do with children's understanding of what we might call the permanence of two. This rhyme could easily be adapted to something more age-appropriate for a pupil with complex needs.

Older infants have been found to retrieve objects they cannot see by making an appropriate number of reaches to bring out each object in turn. They must, therefore, be monitoring the number of items put in a container with the number of items they take out. Thus, what has been seen in young infants as an awareness is used by older infants of 18 months to problem solve.

A famous study by Rochel Gelman further illustrates children's developing understanding. She devised a game called 'winners and losers' – in fact to test, among other skills, young children's understanding of the invariance of number. Children were presented with two saucers holding different set sizes of small toys. The researcher named one saucer the 'winner' and another the 'loser'. The saucers were then covered and shuffled until the children would have lost track of which saucer was where. They were then asked to pick the winner. When the child uncovered a saucer they were asked if it was the winner. Children as young as two years were consistent in their responses – even when the items on the saucer were surreptitiously changed either by adding or subtracting an item or by changing the position of items on the saucer. The success of this activity points to the importance of enabling children to construct their own rules – the adult does not use number words to describe the winner or loser. The activity also provides another example of how children can solve problems using visual perception of number and not have to count.

Our understanding of the way children demonstrate understanding can be used to inform our teaching. The following are illustrations to show the diversity of contexts in which number can be made an important element of early perceptual games. We suggest that identical objects are used if you want to encourage the child to focus on number and not have a perceptual image that 'the blue one has disappeared' or 'where is the tiny trike?' etc. The key aspect is that they draw the child's attention and therefore either they are favourite toys or items or they make a noise, flash and/or move prior to being hidden. For children at the earliest stages, it is likely that the items must continue to emit these qualities even when they are 'hidden'. Research on early cognitive development draws attention to the power of movement and displacement in creating and sustaining interest.

Some early number activities

Hiding two identical favoured objects in the sand/lentils/pasta/jelly while the child watches. Can they find them both? Do they look for the second one?

Submerging two objects under water in the splash pool, then releasing them one at a time to pop up – leaving a pause before the second item to see if the learner shows signs of anticipating the appearance of the second.

Putting an object in one or both hands, hiding them behind your back and then bringing both hands out to see if the child looks in one or both for the desired item.

Using identical objects with a gone box. Do they look for both to reappear?

Playing with the puppet theatre – one puppet appears and talks to the child, a second puppet appears and the curtains close and only one puppet reappears. Are they surprised?

Recent work in school with pupils at this early stage of becoming aware of quantity has highlighted a number of important elements. We had to tune into contexts that were motivating to the individual child and that led to sustained attention, otherwise they would look at one item but would have lost attention before the appearance of the other. It was also vital to take into account the repertoire of responses that the child had at his or her disposal and to use these in a situation where number was relevant and meaningful. For example, if the child's response was to throw or hit items then this had to be built into the 'game'. If the child immediately grabbed, then we had to increase the difficulty of accessing the item to ensure that he or she had time to think before acting. In this study all work was carried out in individual sessions and it is likely that, because of difficulties in gaining and keeping attention, this is the optimum learning situation for some pupils at the initial stages of learning about number.

Key summary points
Infant studies suggest that aspects of the number system develop early with infants of five or six months able to discriminate between sets of two and three when they are presented as:

- two or three objects;
- photographs of two or three items;
- two or three spots.

This discrimination occurs however the items are arranged. Moreover, infants are also able to distinguish between:

- two or three puppet counts;
- two or three sounds.

Infants not only seem to have an *awareness* of numerical differences but it appears as if infants are able to construct mental representations of number as they are also able to *anticipate* the outcome of numerical changes. This perceptual ability is used by older infants to *regulate their actions* and to *problem solve*.

The research suggests that in our teaching we need to:

- use small sets, as children's perceptual processes are best accessed in the early stages using two or three items
- use meaningful concrete activities, ones that hold the child's interest and attention;
- present situations that at the very early stages promote an awareness of differences and then may be linked to anticipation and prediction, before moving on to encourage active problem solving.

Learning about counting
An important distinction has been made between those activities that require language such as counting, and those that do not. Indeed, some researchers have highlighted how the activities are carried out by different halves of the brain, with the right hemisphere responsible for these non-verbal numerical activities and the left for those involving verbal aspects.

Counting can be seen as a verbally based activity in two respects. Firstly, it is the way in which mothers and infants largely interact to produce an activity on which eventually there is an agreed understanding that, for example, there are two shoes, two eyes, one nose and you can have one biscuit! Studies of mothers with typically developing young children have highlighted the ways mothers model number words and number activities that are just a little ahead of their child's abilities. Consensus between mother and child is usually arrived at through language. Work with children who are language impaired or deaf has particularly focused our attention on how children may be deprived of important activities that will support their developing understanding of number. Secondly, and just as importantly, the count sequence is usually learned orally. Research in nursery settings highlights how children are routinely exposed to counting, often as a choral activity, where long number strings are produced in time with putting out drinks and biscuits, counting chairs round the table, putting out equipment, monitoring how many children are playing in a particular area, etc. Children are, therefore, inducted into the world of number and the variety of contexts in which it appears typically through verbal means. Thus, what has started as a non-verbal perceptual ability now has developing alongside it a culturally mediated activity that is verbally based.

One can anticipate already that here may lie many difficulties for pupils with complex needs. If we start with considering the task of learning the number string, then acquisition is dependent on hearing the sequence again and again. There is no predictive pattern of sounds until the child has learned the number string from 1 to 13. The words are learned as a serial list, like learning the alphabet, so that they are acquired as a linked series of sounds, with one number word becoming the cue for the next word in the sequence. Karen Fuson provides us with an outline of the process of acquisition, one that we might identify with if we have recently attempted to learn the words in another language. Initially, for the young child the words are usually learned as a chant with no discernible gap separating the words into distinct units. It is said rather like uttering a rhyme. The child then produces the words so that he or she does make some distinction between one word and the next, but the string continues to be produced as a whole. So, for example, the child always has to start with his first number word, usually one, to produce a count. This is important for teachers to realise as it means that, as they try to help the child to remember what comes next, the child may well find it easier to start the count again. Experienced teachers may even help the child get 'restarted' using a 'chant' if they are at this early stage and experiencing difficulty. Given the child's lack of fluency, it is not surprising that the job of coordinating count words and pointing at objects is beyond the child except for very small sets on which he or she is able to produce the number words with alacrity.

Fuson refers to these two stages as 'chant' and the 'unbreakable chain'. The next stage of acquisition Fuson refers to as the 'breakable chain' as children are now able to produce parts of the count sequence starting at different points – they no longer have to start at one. This has important implications for their counting to objects – they are able to pause in the count process and are able to count on. Two further stages are outlined by Fuson revealing further mental abilities. Children become able to abstract the number words so they can keep track of how many they have uttered, separate to the count process. For example, if we ask the child to count on three from say seven, at this stage they are able to produce the three number words eight, nine and ten whilst keeping track of how many they have uttered. Finally children are able to do this process moving both up and down the sequence of number words. (If you try to move down three numbers in another language, you may appreciate the task demands on memory and attention.)

Stages in Acquiring the Count String: Drawn from Fuson & Hall (1983)
Number words learned first as a chant or song
Children do not fully perceive the gaps between number words and, therefore, are not able to coordinate words with points

Produce a sequence of individual number words but cannot break into the sequence
Children have to begin the count from one (or their first word in the number sequence); they are better able to coordinate pointing with saying the number words

Children are able to break into their sequence, producing parts of the sequence starting at different points
Children can be prompted to produce what comes 'next' and can count on with concrete objects

Children are fluent in their counting and can simultaneously keep track of the number words said
Children can count up three from four, etc., keeping track of the number of number words said

Children can move easily both up and *down* the number chain
Children can count both forwards and backwards through the number word sequence

As we can see from the table above, while learning to produce the number words in sequence is a rote task, our fluency and competence dictate *how* we are able to use that sequence and what other mental operations we are able to carry out at the same time. Therefore, what can be described (and often dismissed) as simply a rote task has implications for the child's learning of other aspects of number. We can also appreciate both the fact that this is commonly a verbally based task and that it makes heavy demands on auditory sequential memory. Both these areas have been cited as possible areas of difficulty for pupils with complex needs. Research carried out with pupils with severe learning difficulties highlighted that this was often a difficult task, especially for the group of pupils with Down syndrome. They may know the number words, but not be able to reliably produce them in the correct order. While children in our research often had the same number vocabulary as nursery-aged pupils their count strings were significantly shorter. If we listen to the counting of some children with complex needs, we can hear that certain words are produced clearly and distinctly, and others are poorly articulated. 'Eight' for example is a nice clear sound to produce, while 'five' may be indistinguishable from 'four'. Again, if we draw a parallel with learning a foreign language, we can understand how difficult it is to remember a word that we have problems pronouncing. If we have some kind of hearing loss, then that sound may be only slightly distinguishable from others.

If children are experiencing particular difficulties with the counting task, there are strong arguments to be made for supporting their learning with visual material: for example, the use of numerical symbols or the use of pictorial representations of the numbers. A parallel to this process is the use of written words to support language development in pupils with Down syndrome. With number, like with words, it is possible to provide cues with the number symbols with dot patterns contained within the symbol.

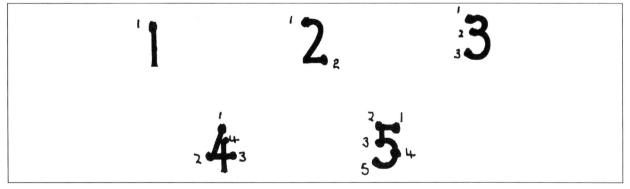

Figure 9.2: Dot patterns as cues to the meaning of number symbols.

Children have to learn the rules of counting in order that the skill becomes a useful tool. Not only do they have to produce the count words in sequence but they also have to use them to tag each item once and once only. They also have to learn that the last number used in the sequence indicates the number of items in the group. It is conventional to make this task as easy as possible for the pupil by placing the items in a line and encouraging them to move sequentially down the line. This helps to reduce the load on memory of recalling which items have been counted and which have not. Experience also indicates that items need to be placed at a suitable distance apart. Too close together and the child is unsure which item he or she has tagged. Too far apart and he or she has to hold onto the next number word in the sequence too long. Some teachers encourage pupils to count while putting items away, but as we have seen, pace is important and if pupils are not fluent then the extra dimension to the activity may distract them.

Research with typically developing children suggests that there may be an order of difficulty whereby children at the earliest stages find objects stuck in a row the easiest situation in which to coordinate the count process. It is not until children are a bit older and more fluent in their production of the number words, that putting objects away elicits more accurate counting. We know from research by Roy McConkey that children with learning difficulties do find it hard to coordinate counting and pointing. Children may, therefore, be best introduced to counting by sharing the task which will enable them to become more fluent in each aspect of it although this should not be at the expense of all solo experience.

It is vital, if children are going to acquire the rules, that the support we give them initially is withdrawn as they become increasingly proficient. While we might start the children using small groups of items in rows and sharing the count process so the child does the tagging and we say the number words (or vice versa) it is important that these arrangements are altered. The child needs to experience counting in a whole variety of contexts if he or she is to realise that the rules of counting do not include putting items out in a row – that this is merely a strategy that he or she may not always need.

Key summary points
- Learning the count word sequence places heavy demands on auditory memory and some children will experience particular difficulties.
- There are a number of stages to the acquisition process and different types of verbal prompting are appropriate at different stages.
- The child's ability to produce count words has a profound effect on how he or she is able to apply them.
- We need to pay attention not just to how many count words the child knows but how fluently he or she can produce these words.
- Some children may be well supported through visual means to supplement oral ways of learning the number words.
- The presentation of items to be counted can impact on how easy the child finds counting but ultimately he or she needs to gain experience of all kinds of counting arrangement.

Understanding cardinality
Cardinality can be understood at many different levels and in many different contexts. At an early level children need to understand that it indicates the number of items in the set, or the number of activities, sounds or events in total. Children may learn that they have two shoes, two gloves, one scarf and thereby be able to use number words as a descriptor. However, they also have to learn the link between counting and cardinality – that we count to find out how many items there are in the group, activities in a day, rings of the bell for the start of school etc. Typically developing children are described as passing through stages whereby they say a single

number after counting but it is not usually the last one uttered (indeed it could be a 'favourite' number). This is followed by a phase of recounting the items when asked how many items, even though they have just counted them. It seems at this stage as if children think that the question 'how many?' is an instruction to count the items. They then return to producing a single digit in answer. The first author's research with pupils with severe learning difficulties suggested that they too followed a similar pattern albeit that there were additional responses made. These included reciting the number words rather than recounting the items. Like mainstream pupils they also responded with a number that was one more or one less than they had reached in their count. Making a variety of responses seems quite a useful indication that the child is actively trying to work out what the correct answer might be – and, therefore, what the rule is.

So how do pupils learn that counting is done to find out how many there are? There seems to be no single answer to this. One way is for adults to explain it and model it for them. Another is to make the connection using small sets which the child is able to visually recognise. Thus, they can see that there are two items and when they count the last number reached is also two. Again, this suggests that children might best learn about counting using small groups of items. Teachers need to measure progress by what they can do and in which contexts rather than focusing on how many numbers the pupil knows.

Having learned that counting is a tool for finding out 'how many?', children then have to learn to use the skill to solve problems. This can be easier said than done as we can see if we think about pupils learning to use counting to make sets. Developmentally this is a considerably more advanced task than being able to count a given set and tell you how many there are. To make a set, one has to hold the target number in mind while counting out items, mentally comparing each number said with the target number. One also has to keep in mind what the requirements of the 'task' are. Children with severe and complex learning difficulties can take a while to learn to use counting in this way – the task is suddenly more difficult. Again, it is likely that children are best helped by keeping set sizes small. This difficulty also reflects the partial understanding that children may have of counting. Research with typically developing five and six year-olds has shown that many are confused if asked how many items would there be if we counted starting at the opposite end of the set or if we counted alternate ones and then came back and counted all the rest. Rochel Gelman has termed this understanding 'the order-irrelevance principle', the understanding that it does not matter what order items are counted in, the number remains the same. This demonstrates how important it is that we do not always expose children to the same conditions for counting as, inadvertently, we may be limiting their developing understanding.

Key summary points
- Children may demonstrate an initial understanding of cardinality through using number words to describe small sets.
- This early labelling may help them to understand counting as a tool for finding out how many.
- Counting is also a tool for making sets but this is both procedurally and conceptually a more advanced task.

Simple arithmetic
Counting is also an important tool for adding and subtracting. It is important that these arithmetic skills are underpinned by understanding of the process. One method of introducing these skills is to encourage the child to mentally represent the process. A seminal study by Martin Hughes involving bricks in a closed tin has been developed and adapted by others to form an informal addition and subtraction activity. The tin, bag or box is shown to the child with a small number of items in, say one or two bricks. The child then sees the addition, or indeed subtraction of items by an adult and, without being able to see the result, has to say how many

items there are now in the container. Research with children whose counting skills are poor provides surprisingly accurate results as they are required by this procedure to mentally represent 'the sum'. In this way children can acquire an understanding of the inverse relationship between subtraction and addition which will underpin their acquisition of more formal procedures.

Once again we have seen the importance of introducing concepts through the use of small numbers of items that children can mentally represent visually. Hughes' studies have revealed how children succeed on this task and make the development to adding when the items have a concrete referent but are not actually there. For example, 'how many are two cups and one cup more?' is solved well before children can respond to 'how many is two and one?', a sum that makes little sense or meaning. Studies of children with learning difficulties suggest that they follow similar stages to mainstream pupils in the development of their strategies for adding and subtracting and, moreover, the development of these strategies is dependent on acquiring the underlying concepts. Children in learning to count two sets of items, for example, count out each of the amounts to be added, the addendum, and then count all the items, starting from one. This is often referred to as 'counting all'. It appears in part to reflect the child's ease with producing the count string for, as we shall see, the next strategy is to 'count on' from the first addendum. Thus, if the child was asked to add two beans and six beans, having counted out each set, he or she would then count on two... three, four, five etc. Finally the child comes to realise that it does not matter which order the addendum are summed, because the answer is the same, and with time will count on from the largest. In the above sum, therefore, the child would add, six... seven, eight. Studies have suggested that this strategy is often elicited first where the sum includes adding one, e.g. adding one car and five cars.

James Hanrahan and Tina Newman suggest that the dot notation numerals can support the transition to adding without the need for concrete items. Thus, pupils would be encouraged to place their pencil or finger on the dots in the symbol while adding two numbers. This, however, raises questions about whether pupils are able to generalise this method and in particular it may be counter-productive when encouraging pupils to acquire strategies for subtraction. Indeed, there is an argument to be made for carefully considering the introduction of symbols in adding and subtracting activities. It is likely that, for many individuals, the importance of these skills lies with their concrete application. In the QCA curriculum guidance for pupils with learning difficulties, an important element of progression is the ability to use these skills in practical settings. Just as we argued that in the earliest stages the child uses their visual perception of quantity to inform their actions and then to actively problem solve, so we can argue that these addition and subtraction strategies should similarly support activities, whether these are leisure pursuits and sports, functional everyday events or other occupations and activities.

The QCA curriculum guidance suggests that we need to place as much emphasis on considering how to ensure that pupils are able to apply their current skills as to the acquisition of new skills. The guidance illustrates how we might think of progression in terms of the pupils developing ability to use mathematical skills and understanding to solve everyday problems. Generalisation also includes the ability to communicate about decisions that use these skills, so that pupils become increasingly able to reflect on their use and are strategic in their application. A vital part of learning involves recognising when the result is surprising and checking that you have not made a mistake, or indeed that somebody else has not made a mistake either.

Key summary points
- *Informal* addition and subtraction can be a useful way of introducing children to these inverse concepts and does not rely on counting skills.

- Children learn to carry out simple arithmetic in practical situations using concrete items and their pictorial equivalents.
- It is important that these skills are used across a range of meaningful contexts as a problem-solving rather than a paper and pencil exercise.

References and useful further reading

Banes, D. (1999) *Spiral Mathematics: Progression and Continuity in Mathematics for Pupils Working Towards Level 1*. Tamworth: NASEN.

Fuson, K. C. (1988) *Children's Counting and Concepts of Number*. New York: Springer-Verlag.

Gelman, R. & Cohen, M. (1988) 'Qualitative differences in the way Down syndrome and normal children solve a novel counting problem', in L. Nadel (Ed.) *The Psychobiology of Down Syndrome*. Mass: M.I.T.

Hanrahan, J. & Newman, T. (1996) 'Teaching Addition to Children', in B. Stratford & P. Gunn (Eds.) *New Approaches to Down Syndrome*. London: Cassell.

Hughes, M. (1986) *Children and Number*. Oxford: Blackwell.

McEvoy, J. & McConkey, R. (1991) 'The performance of children with a moderate mental handicap on simple counting tasks', *Journal of Mental Deficiency Research*, 35, 446–58.

Porter, J. (1999) 'The Attainments of Pupils with Severe Learning Difficulties on a Simple Counting and Error Detection Task', *Journal of Applied Research in Intellectual Disabilities*, 87–89.

Porter, J. (2000) 'The Importance of Creating a Mathematical Environment', *SLD Experience*, 26, 16–17.

QCA (2001) *Planning, Teaching and Assessing the Curriculum for Pupils with Learning Difficulties: Mathematics*. London: QCA.

Staves, L. (2001) *Mathematics of Children with Severe and Profound Learning Difficulties*. London: David Fulton Publishers.

Wynn, K. (1998) 'Numerical Competence in Infants', in C. Donlan (Ed.) *The Development of Mathematical Skills*. E. Sussex: Psychology Press.

Chapter 10: Classroom organisation

It has always been the case that one of the best indicators of teaching quality is the attention that a teacher gives to organising the learning environment. There is now a growing body of literature that recommends a range of practices in the organisation of teaching and learning for children with a range of learning difficulties and this chapter presents some of these ideas. The features emphasised here include the physical organisation of the classroom, the use of visual timetables or schedules and a few teaching methods which rely on deliberately giving visual clues. We have deliberately chosen to talk about features that can be incorporated into the organisation of classrooms in both mainstream schools and special schools.

Physical organisation of the classroom

Few teachers get to choose their classroom or the furniture in it and many have to work within cramped and inadequate schools. There are major issues for governing bodies and local education authorities when it comes to improving the teaching areas in schools. Too many children are taught in classrooms that are too small, that have poor lighting and acoustics, that are remote from the nearest toilets, that lack adequate storage, that have multiple exits which are a magnet for absconders, that lack relatively quiet and distraction-free areas and that are generally spartan. In particular, many schools lack convenient withdrawal areas for children to regain a measure of self-control when they are having difficulty managing their feelings or behaviour. The physical accommodation in most schools is still a vast improvement on that which existed three or four decades ago, but often it does not reflect modern building standards and beliefs about what is necessary to create a relaxed learning atmosphere for children, let alone children with significant learning difficulties.

Nevertheless, there are ways of arranging the physical layout of even these inadequately designed classrooms so that the children's opportunities for learning are significantly enhanced. Proponents of the TEACCH approach stress that rearrangement of the furniture makes it possible to have specific areas for specific learning activities with clear visual boundaries which may be enhanced by improvised screens made of cupboards or marked out by mats and lines on the floor. A teacher of younger children may want to create areas for play as well as for individual and small group work with the teacher or any learning support assistants. In a larger classroom, there may be areas for whole class work and specific areas for books and computers. A classroom for children in their later teenage years might well have specialist equipment and specific areas for teaching 'daily living skills' and for developing leisure activities of various kinds. As well as carefully defining these areas in this way, pupils must learn how they are expected to behave in each particular area of the classroom. So teachers must use the different areas in the special ways that have been designated rather than in ad hoc ways.

Work areas are best situated away from visual distractions, i.e. well away from windows, doors, thoroughfares and mirrors. If necessary, work areas can be hedged around with screens and some windows can be covered over with paper if there are no blinds or curtains. Work areas need to have blank walls – busy and bright displays of work by the children or things for the children to look at are important but should be situated where they do not distract children working. The teaching materials should be in cupboards that are near to or actually in the work areas because there are distractions when the teacher has to fetch them or children have to cross the classroom to get them. Equipment also has to be accessible for those children who are working independently or playing, although it must be equipment that the children can use with supervision rather than strict direction and physical assistance. The location of the equipment in cupboards should be clearly signalled by the use of pictures, symbols or objects of reference on the doors and storage trays.

So there are a number of questions that teachers need to consider when they are arranging the physical layout of their classroom. Are there distinctive areas for teaching individuals and small groups of children and have all potential distractions been removed or minimised? Are there defined areas for children to play and are they big enough? Will the teacher or a learning support assistant have clear sight of these areas and what is going on in any other nooks and crannies in the room? Are there small areas for children to work independently or sit and read or even just to sit quietly for a few moments of their own? Is the location of equipment clearly marked, are children able to access the equipment they may need and is the equipment they should not have firmly shut away? Can the classroom computer and other expensive and breakable equipment be shut way or at least covered up when an adult cannot supervise its use? Has the clutter of rarely used or unnecessary equipment and materials been removed from the classroom to create as much available space as possible? Can children and staff freely traverse the classroom without interrupting teaching activities or other work that is ongoing?

Using pictures in association with reward systems

Every teacher prefers to work with children who are well motivated and good teachers will make judicious use of words of encouragement and explicit, positive feedback. However, for some children with learning difficulties, these are simply not strong enough motivators or are not understood. More material rewards, such as favourite activities or toys, are often used because they provide the immediate and explicit feedback that some children with profound learning difficulties require. However, over time, it is desirable to increase the amount of work expected of a child before getting the reward. One way of deferring gratification, but keeping children motivated, is to introduce a visual representation of how much more they need to do before getting the material reward.

Paul has a reward card that bears three circles. Each time that Paul completes an activity he is praised by his teacher and given a smiley face token that he sticks in one of the circles. When all three circles are filled in, Paul eagerly hands over the card to get his reward. He chooses this from a box containing things that he is known to like especially: a Walkman with headphones, a pack of picture cards, jigsaws, a computer game, etc.

It took a lot of prior work to get Paul to this stage. Initially, he was given access to the reward box each time he completed an activity. As a next step, he was given a token after completing the activity and was prompted to trade for his reward. This continued until he was consistently handing over the token for his reward without any prompts. As a third step, as soon as he completed the activity, he was given the token and prompted to stick it on the reward card which he was prompted to hand over to get his toy. After some time at this stage, a reward card with two circles was introduced and he was required to complete two activities before getting his reward. He is now at the stage where he will complete three activities without demur because he has a visual reminder of what he is working to achieve. In the future, it may be possible to increase the number of circles to five or more, but Paul's teacher is keen that he should receive a reward at least two or three times during the course of each day.

Of course, Paul has not always worked for the same rewards. There were times when his attention waned and it was found that a different reward needed to be added to the box.

Teaching independent working

A major feature of the TEACCH approach to teaching children with autism has been the use of visual schedules with individuals to support the development of their independent working skills. They can help children to understand what work they have to do, the sequence of activities and when they are finished. They can also free up teachers and learning support assistants for more time to be spent on the teaching of new skills to others. The ideal goal is that each child will eventually follow some kind of personal schedule showing the independent work activities to be done by him or her. When teaching children to work independently, the activities must be familiar and the skills required to complete them should have been learned previously. Independent work should not be used to teach new skills other than the skills of working independently. Of course, many children will require supervision and support from a teacher for learning the routines of independent working. However, the teacher's presence and any verbal reminders and physical cues should be faded as soon as possible.

As described in Chapter 7, when it comes to the 'work' activity on the general class timetable, individualised activities for children may be displayed on each child's own schedule. Some independent learning activities may take place at a workstation. The workstation may simply be a table in a relatively quiet corner or the teacher may set up a screen around a table using cardboard sheets or more solid screens in order to cut down on sources of distraction for the child. The number of children who may do independent working at workstations simultaneously depends on the number of children and staff, the resources available and the size of the room. Most likely, there will only be one or two children working independently, while others are being supervised in general activities or are being directly taught new skills. The specific arrangements depend upon the teacher knowing the children and what works, given the human and physical resources available. One teacher might be able to work directly with one child at one workstation while keeping an eye on a child working independently at a neighbouring workstation, for instance. Alternatively, an adult may teach new skills to a child and then back away a little while the child works independently at other activities.

A left-to-right work routine can be a helpful routine. There should be work boxes containing the work that each child has to complete, perhaps with the materials for each activity kept separately in zipped, clear bags. The workboxes are probably best located in a cupboard by the workstation. If located in a central resource, there are many distractions for the children if they have to leave their work station to fetch the next box. It makes sense to start with just one or two bags of work and gradually increase the number according to the ability of the individual child to maintain concentration and perseverance. The box of bags is placed on the child's left-hand side in the workstation and an empty box is placed on the right-hand side. The work routine proceeds as follows:

- child selects first bag from box on the left-hand side and does activity;
- child puts work back in bag and puts it in the box on right side of workstation when work is finished;
- child repeats process with next bag of work;
- when all work is finished, all work should be packed away in bags and should be in the box on the right side;
- child shows teacher that work is done, teacher checks, child is allowed to choose an activity or other reward.

The number of bags and the degree of supervision required will vary from child to child, of course. Incidentally, there is no reason why the same pattern of left-to-right working should not be adopted when teaching new skills; this would seem to be a sensible reinforcement of the routine.

One goal is that children work independently on a range of activities. The TEACCH approach allows for workboxes, or bags, to be marked in a specific way, e.g. a photo, picture, dab of colour, numeral, as appropriate to the individual child's level of understanding. The child's own schedule can, therefore, contain corresponding markers to indicate the workboxes, or bags, to be worked through and the sequence in which to do it. The markers may be used as follows:

- child takes first marker from schedule showing activity to be done and finds workbox/bag with corresponding marker;
- completes task, puts box/bag on right;
- takes next marker and repeats process;
- the child knows that the work has finished when all markers are gone from schedule and may seek a chosen activity as reward.

The left-to-right sequence and the markers are visual cues that may be faded in the fullness of time. However, even children who are working at a relatively advanced level may benefit from having access to a simple work schedule showing tasks to be done. This could be kept in a personal planner or diary, which may be a series of pages in a ring binder, for instance. Then it is simply a case of the child checking off each item as the activity is completed.

Of course, not all independent work has to take place in a workstation. Much independent working can occur in a variety of other settings if the same general principles are adopted. Left-to-right routines and task organisers, as described in Chapter 7, may help children to perform a whole range of tasks independently or with reduced levels of supervision. However, the consistent message is that preparation of visual schedules and task organisers depends upon careful analysis of the learning task and ensuring that the children have been carefully and thoroughly taught how to do the activities before they are taught to do them independently.

High/Scope
High/Scope developed from work undertaken with disadvantaged pre-schoolers in the USA in the 1960s and 1970s. It has been used in mainstream primary schools and nurseries in this country and Suzie Mitchell has written about the possible applications of the High/Scope approach to children with learning difficulties. It deserves a mention because it systematically incorporates visual clues and routines, but there is an emphasis upon active learning and problem solving which is not so apparent in the TEACCH approach. Indeed, as mentioned in the first chapter, there have been criticisms that the TEACCH approach provides such a specialised environment to meet the particular needs of children with autism that there are inherent dangers that they are not stretched enough: teachers do need to think very carefully about how to sufficiently prepare children for situations in which they have to think for themselves, to make choices, to learn from their mistakes, to function without adult-imposed structures and so on. High/Scope uses the space available in the classroom carefully: by careful arrangement of the furniture, areas are designated for particular purposes (e.g. painting, imaginative play, writing, reading); the storage for equipment is accessible by the children (unless the equipment is for adult-supervised activities only); the children are expected to tidy up the equipment when they have finished with it and they can do this because everything is labelled (e.g. by pictures, symbols and/or words) and has its own place. Active learning and problem solving are given great emphasis: the children are encouraged to make choices about what activities they are going to do, to carry out their work plans and to discuss them with their peers and the adults present. The day is divided into a sequence of PLAN-DO-REVIEW routines: they plan with an adult what they are going to do; they do the activity; they tidy up; and with the adult they review what they have done.

There is no reason why the PLAN-DO-REVIEW routines cannot be used with many children with learning difficulties of all ages. In fact, it seems that the routines could fit in well with the structures recommended for whole class, group and individual work for the Literacy Hour and mathematics time. Due to their language and cognitive difficulties, the range of choices may have to be limited, but choice making can be supported by the use of visual displays of symbols for the available activities. At review time, signs and symbols that indicate 'like', 'dislike' and so on can support evaluations. If the pupil:adult ratios are favourable, there may be opportunities for adults to work with individuals and small groups on their chosen activities and to keep their own records as well as examples of the pupils' work that is generated.

Key summary points

There are a range of ways in which the classroom environment can be organised to create visually different areas for specific activities.

- Work areas for teaching skills or for independent working should have visual and other distractions reduced as much as possible.
- General classroom timetables and individual pupil timetables are essential.
- Left-to-right routines and work schedules can be used to help establish independent working.
- PLAN-DO-REVIEW routines could help encourage truly independent working.

References and useful further reading

Bondy, A. & Frost, L. (1994) *The Picture Exchange Communication System Training Manual.* Cherry Hill, NJ: Pyramid Educational Consultants.

Hodgdon, L. A. (1995) *Visual Strategies for Improving Communication – Volume 1: Practical Supports for Home and School.* Troy, Michigan: Quirk Roberts Publishing. Available from Winslow Press.

Hohmann, M. & Weikart, D. P. (1995) *Educating Young Children: active learning practices for pre-school and child care programs.* Michigan: High/Scope Press.

Mitchell, S. (1994) 'Some implications of the High/Scope curriculum and the education of children with learning difficulties', in J. Coupe O'Kane and B. Smith (Eds) *Taking Control.* London: David Fulton Publishers.

Watson, L., Lord, C., Schaffer, B. & Schopler, E. (1987) *Teaching Spontaneous Communication to Autistic and Developmentally Handicapped Children.* Austin, Texas: Pro-ed. Available from Winslow Press.

Chapter 11: Multisensory environments

There has been a tremendous growth in the use of multisensory environments since the 1970s but not without a considerable amount of controversy and debate. Their origins are usually quoted as lying with the introduction of Snoezelen rooms in residential settings. The opportunities provided in these early sensory rooms for safe and relaxing recreation were quickly recognised in what was often an otherwise impoverished environment. Increasingly schools have sought to capitalise on their educational potential but, as we shall see, research does not currently support their indiscriminate use. Nevertheless, in many settings they have been established as a result of considerable fund-raising and it is important to reflect on how they might be used to best effect.

The term 'multisensory environments' is used to describe a whole range of provision. Paul Pagliano lists a total of 12 types, including the less common (at least currently in the UK) virtual environment where 3-D interactive computer imaging provides access to an alternative world. Other types are likely to be more familiar to the reader. Probably the most common form of multisensory environment is a white room in which 2-D visual effects can be screened. The contrast to this is a dark room in which visual stimuli can be presented in a distraction-free environment. Pagliano's list also includes soft play areas; a sound space for the presentation of enhanced auditory stimuli; and a water area where lights, Jacuzzi, slides and waterfalls can promote movement in the supportive environment of water.

In addition to these high-tech and sometimes extravagantly designed spaces that may extend to a suite of rooms, there are also the low tech options, home-made corners of rooms or cupboards, designed and constructed by individual members of staff. While these might provide crowded and cramped working conditions, they may have a number of distinct advantages over the more expensive environments. These settings are often constructed a step at a time by trial and error. Restrictions in space means that they include what works and adapt what does not. Rather than being filled with static equipment that dominates and may even need protecting from certain children, the space may be highly mobile and flexible and can be reconstructed for particular needs. It is possible therefore that these low tech options are often more child-led in their design.

Given the range of provision, what do these multisensory environments have in common? Perhaps the best description is that they form a distraction-free location for staff to provide controlled use of stimulation, targeted to the needs of particular children, often individually but sometimes as a group. The name 'multisensory environments' is a misnomer, as it suggests that they are there to provide stimulation to more than one sense at a time. Indeed, the implication is the more senses the better! There is considerable debate about this, given that children often have difficulty taking in information from more than one sense at a time and that coordinating information from two senses may pose particular difficulties for children, depending on their attentional control. Schools often use a range of terms to label these environments, one of the most popular being 'interactive environment', sensibly drawing attention to the importance of enabling the child to be active and in control of gaining stimulation.

Robert Orr is well quoted in stating:

'Students have been observed withdrawing psychologically from the overwhelming battery of lights and unfathomable sequences of events.'

(Orr, 1999/2000, p.6)

Just as contentiously, he also expresses concern that people will ignore the sensory properties of the natural world in favour of the 'funfair' of the multisensory environment.

This chapter will be concerned with identifying good practice. It draws on research carried out by the first author and Olga Miller in a project funded by the British Educational Communications and Technology Agency (BECTA) on the use of technology. The project involved setting up a focus group of professionals working across a range of settings with pupils with complex needs. We also made a number of case study visits in which we had the privilege of observing pupils in a whole range of multisensory environments and of discussing their learning with staff. While the particular focus in this book is on practices that promote learning through visual access, these environments, if carefully used, provide an important resource in a whole variety of additional ways.

First let us consider the range of uses. Elsewhere we have pointed to the importance of clarity of purpose and it is with this in mind that the following list of uses was created:

- the development of the senses; although vision predominates as Pagliano's list indicates, provision is also made for sound, touch, smell and kinaesthesis;
- assessment of the use of senses;
- promoting an understanding of cause and effect;
- developing choices;
- a social space for promoting interaction;
- developing independent movement and exploration of materials;
- as a therapeutic environment for pupils with challenging behaviour;
- as a dramatic backdrop for promoting access to curriculum areas;
- developing understanding of the use of technology.

It is not intended that this list is exhaustive (Richard Byers, for example, also refers to self-awareness, empowerment and relaxation), but rather serves to prompt increased awareness of the range of purposes. Depending on the aim, the environment will be utilised in vastly different ways. As others have stated, work outside the environment should also reflect the use that is made of it. Many teachers we talked to spoke of the environment acting as a catalyst, kick-starting a pupil's awareness and providing the staff with important information that would shape provision in the wider environment.

Good practice in the use of multisensory environments is only tenuously linked to specific research. Reviews of the literature have highlighted the limitations of research reflecting in part the difficulties of larger-scale studies evaluating specific forms of intervention with children with complex needs. James Hogg concludes that there is at present no conclusive research that demonstrates the effectiveness of these environments. He points to the marked individual variation in the way people responded. Anecdotal evidence, in contrast, provides convincing and often heartfelt descriptions of the way that individuals have changed as a result of experiences in a multisensory environment. McCormack, for example, described how her daughter was previously unresponsive 'to any stimulation provided to her... [she] was living in a world closed by her severe limitations.' She took her daughter for a session in a multisensory environment and 'like magic' her daughter 'opened up and responded to the total sensory environment that the room enveloped her in'.

Such dramatic personal stories highlight the need for teachers to provide their own evidence, to carefully monitor both their actions and the presence and absence of pupils' responses.

Part of the difficulty in assessing the evidence lies with identifying the theoretical basis for the use of multisensory environments. One of the areas in which they are most widely used is that of visual stimulation and visual training. There has been considerable debate about the development of vision and in particular the role of visual stimulation. While the jury is still out on the plasticity of the brain and the ability to stimulate the brain in receiving visual messages, medical opinion favours the likelihood of there being an age ceiling of about eight years on the possibility of promoting new visual pathways. For many of the youngsters, the nature of their visual impairment is likely to be cortical, that is to say that the eyes appear normal in their functioning but the messages are not received or interpreted by the brain. It is estimated that this is the most predominant form of visual impairment in school-aged pupils and presents the most complex pattern. Judicious use of visual stimulation may enable the teacher to identify the conditions in which the pupil most reliably responds to visual information. For example, it may enable the teacher to identify which colours the pupil can see (these are often, but not always, at the red end of the spectrum), whether they need to hold an object before they can see it, whether they use peripheral rather than central vision and whether they have figure-ground confusions that can only be resolved by getting close to an item.

For other pupils the environment may be used to train their use of residual vision. Natalie Barraga (and others) have developed hierarchies of skills based on the normal development of vision although there is some debate about whether the 'stages' need to be rigidly followed. We know from tests of infant development, for example, that high contrast, low density black and white stripes presented centrally attract gaze and as acuity develops, more complex visually dense items are fixated on. As their attention and acuity develops, infants more naturally respond to moving rather than stationary objects. Among the dangers of using developmental scales are that they take no account of meaning and motivation. Thus, an object may be visually difficult to discriminate but still located by the child over considerable distances because it signals an important event or because it is highly desirable in its own right. On occasions, visual training in a natural environment will have many advantages, not least because the use of environmental sounds and movements may alert the child to the significance of the item which cannot be usefully manufactured in an artificial environment.

Positioning is a vital element in the effective use of multisensory environments. There are two, often contradictory, aspects to take into account. For vision and sound, the nearer to upright the position, the easier we are able to locate the source of the stimulation. However, we must be in a position that does not demand attention to maintain, otherwise we are distracted. For many children with physical difficulties we may need to compromise. A deciding factor may be whether the position facilitates the pupil's ability to control the stimuli through, for example, easy contact with the source or with a switch.

The multisensory environment may be used with some individuals to promote a reaching response or grasp an object. The advantage of a multisensory environment can be that it provides a distraction-free setting in which an attention-grabbing object can be presented in a way that motivates the pupil to reach out. In the following scenario the teacher presents fluorescent sticks under an ultraviolet light in a dark room.

The teacher is working with two pupils. They are singing a song while banging the bright rods together. Vijay holds a rod in each hand and brings them together in midline. He moves them apart and one drops from his hand. He reaches out to grasp a different coloured one from the teacher's outstretched hand.

The aim is for Vijay to reach for the rods, and to release them. As the teacher says, that is particularly difficult for him because of his cerebral palsy.

'... In class he doesn't do so well. When he's holding his spoon he can't release but in there he often ... does release.'

Orr highlights the necessity of staff considering the effectiveness of their actions. An important element in the effective use of a multisensory environment is for staff to be clear about their role. In the previous examples, the multisensory environment has been selected as a context for working because it is distraction-free. It provides an optimum setting for carefully targeted presentation of stimuli. Where the focus is to build the child's awareness of visual stimuli, the adult might prove a distraction, diverting concentration from the task, for example through shifting the child's visual attention to their movements or shifting the child's awareness to the aural stimulus of their voice.

The adult must, therefore, complement this rather than produce competing stimuli. Language may be inappropriate as, after all, we may want him or her to be interacting with the environment rather than with us. In this context it may be particularly important to ensure that any interruptions are kept to a bare minimum.

For other pupils, the aim of using the multisensory environment may be to encourage social interaction. Orr (1999/2000, p.7) describes how he:

'observed a session where the teacher held a limp child close to her and breathed in and out at the same pace as the child who, for the first time, lifted her head and made eye contact...'

This illustration shows the power of shared attention – the very basis of developing communication. If the aim is to encourage social interaction then these environments can provide an enabling context, one in which the adult is able to follow the child's attention and build social routines. In this situation the adult forms an important element in a responsive environment. Important techniques will include not only giving the pupil time to respond but also for them to 'ask', intercepting their eye-gaze to promote a functional communicative response.

We have considered the role of adults in promoting a responsive environment. However, it is also important for children to realise that *they* can have an impact, that they are not reliant on others to make things happen for them. Again this has important implications for the role of the adult who acts as an enabler for the child to make this connection. An advantage of the multisensory environment over a part of the classroom is simply that it can provide controlled conditions in which the outcome of activating a switch is clearly discernible. It is the distraction-free nature of an environment and the ability to enhance the effects that encourage the child to make a connection between his or her actions and a particular outcome. Russell, for example, was observed activating the sound of himself laughing with a Big Mac switch. The effect was enhanced by the use of an amplifier which made the sound louder and improved its quality.

The selection of the switch is important, together with finding the best outcome for the pupil. For example, if the switch is hand operated it needs to be sensitive not just to the pressure but the type of movement characteristic of the child and located in a position that is most readily 'discovered' by the child.

Vivish is enjoying the feel of the bubble tube; he has his cheek pressed against it. There are two tubes on in an otherwise darkened room. One of the bubble tubes goes off and the room visibly darkens. Vivish stills, then after a few moments moves his hand towards the switch; he knocks it but nothing happens. The teacher immediately leans over and guides him to try again, making the necessary flick action so that the second bubble tube lights the room.

After this session the teacher talked about it with us.

'He was actually enjoying the bubble tube so it was nice to see him realising when it was switched off and he was locating the switch... he was feeling where the switch was... I've found that it's the most successful switch... that one works best because it works with his flick action.'

The switch selected had a timed action so that the effect lasted for some 20 seconds, then stopped with an opportunity for the child to repeat the action. The alternative modes – momentary, where the effect lasts as long as the contact, and latch, where the movement turns the switch on like a light switch – were felt to be inappropriate for the child's learning needs at this point. Once Vivish has reliably made a connection he may be taught to use a second switch for a different event. He will be then in a position to make a choice. It is noticeable in our vignette that the member of staff does not distract the child by talking to them and waits for them to make a response before intervening.

It is important to consider the longer-term aims in designing a programme of teaching. One teacher in our study described her choice of switch for a tactile defensive pupil as one that was part of a secondary aim to encourage him to use his hands:

'He had a similar switch which he used as a head switch but it's not the way I want [him] to go... he needs to use his hands... because having no vision its very, very important... it doesn't need a lot of pressure so that he can rest his hand and trigger it.'

The switch is used with the most motivating event that they can find for him – excerpts from opera, to which he clearly demonstrates his appreciation and about which he is very discerning. Again, the role of the adult lies with supporting him to make this link. When the music stops, she waits for him to make a response and then gently supports his elbow and releases it so that his hand makes contact with the switch.

Multisensory environments have been used for children with a variety of challenging behaviours. While research in this area generally suffers the same limitations of poor design leading to inconclusive findings, their use does rest on proven theory of some of the variables that can contribute to the development of challenging behaviour. Research has, for example, pointed to the role of sensory stimulation in contributing to stereotyped and self-injurious behaviours. Interestingly, some challenging behaviours have been seen as resulting from both under-stimulation and over-stimulation, indicating the importance of children being able to control the amount of stimulation they receive. Challenging behaviour in other children has been linked to the response of the adult, either because staff provide an aversive stimulus, such as in the presentation of tasks, which is to be avoided, or because the behaviour elicits a desired response such as attention. Individual pupils present distinct profiles and, therefore, it is with this caution in mind that we describe good practice.

Access to these environments should not be contingent on the behaviour in the sense that one should not reliably (or unreliably) follow the other. Their use is not to provide a reward or as a time out room, tempting though it is to use them to restore peace and calm for the staff and pupils left behind in the classroom! Rather it is an unthreatening environment for exploration and investigation where the pupil can access alternative forms of stimulation through positive interaction. The environment should be relaxing and the pupil should be in control rather than have demands made by staff (or indeed other pupils). Interestingly, research has almost unanimously suggested that multiple forms of stimulation should be available. However, this does not suggest that they should all be activated at once, rather that they should be used to entice the pupil to investigate. The focus has always been on measuring pupil changes in behaviour (e.g. chooses activity, initiates contact, verbalises, explores, etc.) but the use of this room may also be beneficial to staff in helping them to regain confidence and start to restore positive interactions.

The chapter would not be complete without some reference to the ways in which the multisensory environment is also being used in curriculum specific ways. For example, it can provide a dramatic context for developing an understanding of an experience that would otherwise be outside the reach of the pupils. This includes historical or literary settings where the imaginative use of the technology can recreate scenes from other contexts. Indeed, pupils themselves can be encouraged to consider how to utilise the technology to produce particular effects. In this way the environments can be a catalyst for the development of a much broader range of skills and understanding.

Key summary points
- Staff need to be clear about the purpose of using a multisensory environment, with an eye on the longer-term aims.
- The purpose shapes the selection of equipment and the way in which it is used.
- The purpose also provides the point of reference for the role of staff themselves.
- Work in the multisensory environment should be clearly linked to teaching provision outside.
- The environment is a tool, best used where the child is active and in control.
- Access can be promoted through considered positioning of the equipment as well as the individual.

References and useful further reading

Barraga, N. (1974) 'Perceptual development in low vision children: a practical approach', *Proceedings of the Australian and New Zealand Association of Teachers of the Visually Handicapped Conference*, 1-10. Brisbane, Australia: ANZAEVH.

Bozic, N. & Murdoch, H. (1996) *Learning through Interaction: Technology and Children with Multiple Disabilities*. London: David Fulton Publishers.

Byers, R. (1998) 'Sensory Environments – for pupils with profound and multiple learning difficulties: innovations in design and practice', *PMLD Link*, 32, 28–31.

Hogg, J. (2000) 'Does Snoezelen Work? Research findings and issues in the envaluation of multisensory techniques', *Journal of Intellectual Disability Research,* 44, 3 & 4, p.527. New Millenium Research to Practice Congress Abstracts. 11th World Congress of the International Association for the Scientific Study of Intellectual Disabilities (IASSID) 1–6 August, 2000, Seattle, Washington, USA.

McCormack, B. (2000) 'How Snoezelen affected the life of my daughter: A mother's story', *Journal of Intellectual Disability Research,* 44, 3 & 4, p.387. New Millenium Research to Practice Congress Abstracts. 11th World Congress of the International Association for the Scientific Study of Intellectual Disabilities (IASSID) 1–6 August, 2000, Seattle, Washington, USA.

Orr, R. (1999) 'Using multisensory environments', *PMLD Link* 1999/2000, 12, 2, pp.6–7.

Pagliano, P. (1999) *Multisensory Environments*. London: David Fulton Publishers.

Porter, J. & Miller, O. (2000) 'Developing the use of multisensory environments', *PMLD Link* 1999/2000, 12, 8–11. See also the BECTA website: www.becta.gov.org/inclusion/sen/resources/multisensory.

Chapter 12: Evaluation

Throughout the book we have highlighted the importance of using teaching approaches that access learning through visually based methods, including number, the development of communication systems such as signs and symbols, approaches to reading and to providing cues in the classroom environment. We have not, however, proposed that these methods are a panacea for all pupils with complex needs, nor that it is the only approach that can be effective. In part, this reflects our knowledge of individual pupils but it also arises from our keen awareness of the limitations in research evidence. Increasingly there is a demand for quantitative data, for scientific proof that will support teachers in the selection of their approaches. Interestingly, one of the areas of particular research centres on work carried out with children with Down syndrome where visual methods to developing language have been well documented. The use of signs and symbols and other alternative communication systems has also been the subject of some research. In most cases, however, the empirical evidence is limited.

The reasons for this are many. In the field of complex needs, evaluative research poses a number of difficulties. To prove that a particular method works calls for comparison to other methods in controlled settings. Teachers naturally adapt methods in line with their own style of teaching, so methods in this way become to some extent personalised. Changes will also occur in the context of how the pupil responds. Often these differences are subtle although there will be a point at which adaptations violate some of the fundamental principles on which an approach is based. A controlled study will require the parameters of an approach to be clearly set out, and teachers to be trained in following the core principles of an approach. If we are to formally compare approaches, this structure will also need to be true of a second method.

In order to be able to generalise the data, we need to establish a representative sample. This is problematic in relation to pupils with complex needs where there is no easily identifiable group. This is very evident when we look at surveys carried out by Dawn Male of the wide-ranging populations to be found in schools for children with severe and moderate learning difficulties. It is perhaps hardly surprising that the methods have often been evaluated with respect to one of the largest group of pupils who are the most easy to identify, pupils with Down syndrome. This in itself is problematic as it assumes greater homogeneity within this group of pupils than across pupils with different etiology. Given the variation in the way Down syndrome is expressed, this can lead to false assumptions and stereotypes.

It is unlikely that researchers will develop methodologies based on random control trials of the type favoured by the DfES and some of the research funding bodies. Apart from logistical difficulties there are also important ethical issues that researchers would face. The selection of pupils for a particular approach is characteristically based on need in special education. Having identified a need, teachers will feel a moral duty to ensure that as far as possible those needs are met. Access to appropriate teaching on the basis of developing a research methodology is not easily compatible with a child-centred approach to learning. While there are methodologies that would meet some of these criticisms, they can be cost and time-intensive and researchers encounter particular difficulties in gaining funding for what are considered minority groups of pupils.

There is, however, often powerful anecdotal evidence that supports the use of these methods, together with a strong underlying rationale which is based on empirical studies of the strengths and difficulties in the learning process encountered by different groups of students. It is likely that, if special education methods were confined to that for which there was widespread and largely unequivocal proof of its success, teachers would be severely restricted in the methods they use. However, it is essential that, as a profession, we are not seen to be climbing on the latest bandwagon and that we do at least individually evaluate how effective our approach is. Teacher evaluation avoids some of the difficulties inherent in larger-scale studies. Firstly, the focus of interest is the particular pupil or group of pupils. The aim is not usually to be able to generalise to unknown groups. Secondly, the process has a particular validity as it is based on naturally occurring contexts rather than those that have been artificially created.

Indeed, as we shall see, teacher evaluation is a vital part of raising the profile of teaching as a profession.

Teacher evaluation

Evaluation is often confused with assessment, yet the two processes, although related, are also quite distinct in what they try to discover. They might be better described as two interrelated processes. The process and methods of assessment are far better documented. Test this out. Pick up a book on special needs and turn to the back to look in the index. It is noticeable that assessment features much more often than evaluation. Furthermore when both are included, more pages are devoted to assessment than to evaluation and yet both are integral to the teaching process. What are the differences between the two? Do we really need evaluation?

They form two complementary processes in developing our professional practice. Assessment is of no use if it does not inform practice. Evaluation is superficial if it is not based on assessment of pupil progress.

Assessment typically focuses on the pupil and asks the questions: What can they do? and What can they do now that they could not do before? Evaluation, however, seeks to find out what has prompted this change: Does this method work? It forms an essential part of thinking about our teaching. The danger with including only assessment is that we focus purely on the difficulties that the child is encountering and we do not consider that in some way we might actually be compounding that difficulty. Evaluation, therefore, is a risky business as it demands that we examine our own practice – both the good and the bad! However, it also requires that we go further and analyse what it was that was good and what it was that was bad.

The two processes, therefore, form a sequence in our decision making. Day-to-day evaluation of teaching strives to answer the question: What learning is taking place? Is the child making progress? To this we add the questions: What supports the child's progress? How will this inform my teaching? These are not easy questions to answer and demand of teachers good observation skills of both the pupil(s) and themselves and reflection on the implications of these observations.

In the context of this book we need to particularly ask:
What *sense* was utilised in the presentation of this task?
What type of response was required?

Paul Pagliano in his book on multisensory environments provides in the appendix a list of some of the dimensions to consider in the presentation of different stimuli. We can draw on some of these here in relation to evaluating visual access systems. First let us consider aspects of the task presentation. They include elements that are specific to the *nature of the visual stimuli* used such as size, intensity, colour, lighting conditions. We also need to consider whether they are accompanied by *other cues* – the use of language or other oral cues, touch or other tactile cues, actions that might be felt as opposed to observed. We also need to consider other elements of the *learning context* – the experience of being in a group and the size and composition of the group as opposed to individual work. We might also want to consider some *pupil characteristics* of a particular session – the pupils' level of energy, their arousal and motivation.

What are important aspects to note about the way the pupil responded? As we have already indicated, we need to consider what type of response was expected and made – was it oral, visual, gestural, a particular action or a more general response? How quickly did it occur? Did the pupil look for feedback while they were responding or was it produced confidently? Did the teacher have to encourage or elicit the response and, if so, how did this occur? Did the teacher show the pupil what to do or give him or her verbal clues?

In the following vignettes we illustrate the way in which sessions have been evaluated. We have included narrative observations to provide the reader with a fuller description of the teaching sessions. These have then been summarised in a format that could be used in the classroom. It would, of course, be possible to make even briefer records; for example, if we simply wanted to monitor the pupils' responses and conclude whether or not the approach was successful in bringing about learning. However, teaching is a more complex business than simply applying a set of techniques, or using a particular piece of equipment. It is, therefore, important to include information that helps us to see the child's response in the broader context of what actions and responses the teacher made.

Observation 1: Using a multisensory environment to teach colour
The teacher (T) and two lads, David and Paul, are sitting by the infinity box, in a darkened multisensory environment. Both boys have particular difficulty in retaining the name of the primary colours. There are three switches in front of them which glow in the dark. Depressing the switch will change the colour of the lights in the infinity box accordingly. The session starts with naming the switches.

> T: *Now then, David, can you find me the RED switch, the red switch? Look at them all carefully.*
> David moves towards the yellow switch.
> T: *Is that the red one?*
> David tries to press the switch.
> T: *Nothing is going to happen. I want you to find me the red switch.*
> David touches the red one.
> T: *Well done. What colour?*
> David: *It's red.*
> T: *So when I say find me the red switch ... you're going to...*
> David touches the red switch.
> T: *Paul, can you find me the blue switch?*
> Paul moves towards it.
> T: *Where's the blue switch?*
> Paul touches it.
> T: *Very good. Blue. Now David, find me the red switch.*
> David touches it.
> T: *What colour is it?*
> David: *Blue.*
> T: *R...*
> David: *Red.*
> T: *Red switch.*

At this point we can see that, although David has named the red switch correctly once, he has also called it blue and only corrected himself when prompted by the teacher. The session continues by using the switch to make the visual light display (an infinity tunnel) light up with the same colour lights as the switch.

T: *Now what's going to happen when you press that red switch? What colour will you get? A red switch will make a …?*
David: *Aah.*
T: *A red light.*
David: *Red.*
T: *Switch it on then and see if it will work.*
David presses switch.
T: *What colour's that light then?*
David switches light on and off repeatedly.
David: *It's blue.*
T: *It's r…*
David: *Red.*
T: *Red. How many red lights can you see… lots…?*
David leans back and presses another switch without looking.
T: *What's that one?*
David: *Bl… Looks back at it. Green.*
T: *Blue… you were right the first time.*
Teacher moves David's hand towards another switch.
T: *And what's this one?*
David: *Red.*
T: *Y…*
David: *Yellow.*

At the end of this session we can see that David is still quite confused about colour. Below we have transformed this narrative observation into a more conventional way of recording the session. This shows that David has not correctly identified the colour of the lights without help. It appears then that the infinity tunnel may not be helping. However, we must ask a number of other questions. Is he thinking before he responds to the colour of the lights? Will he self-correct without the prompts of the teacher? Is he looking at the switch before pressing it to link the switch colour and the light colour? Is he distracted by the responses of the other pupil?

Table 12.1:

Context	Task	Pupil Response	Teacher Response to pupil
Location: Multisensory environment Organisation: 1 to 2 Materials: Red, yellow and blue switches that glow in dark	Find … (choice of 3) Name … (choice of 3) Find … (choice of 3)	Touches yellow Touches red Says red Touches red	Asks question Asks question Recap
Red switch	Name … (choice of 3)	Blue Red	Verbal prompt Allows to press
Red light	Name … (choice of 3)	Blue Red	Verbal prompt Asks question
Blue light		Green	Corrects answer
Yellow light		Red Yellow	Verbal prompt

76

The teacher in evaluating the pupil's response in relation to the teaching goes on to introduce an activity which is designed to make David think further about the colour. First, they stick the corresponding colour symbols on to the switch. David has no difficulty with this matching task. They then turn the switches over so the cue is the colour symbol. David is asked again to 'Find the one that makes red.' David succeeds in doing this. However, when asked subsequently to name the colour of the lights, he gets it wrong. In fact, on closer scrutiny, when the infinity tunnel lights up yellow, other coloured bulbs can be seen. Is it possible that despite the fact that it is highly motivating for David to press the switch, the activity is in fact confusing? On looking around at other equipment, it can be seen that the bubble tubes light up with purer and distinctive colours and, therefore, might be a better medium. It may, however, also be that David could be helped by being given verbal cues. For example, reference to a favourite football team and the colour of their strip might help David to associate the name with the colour better. In conclusion, while the multisensory environment provides a new and attractive way to teach David, not all equipment is equally appropriate and the teacher might also consider the use of verbal cues to encourage him to make visual links.

Observation 2: Developing awareness of quantity

The teacher is sitting across the table from Sandy to encourage her to join in a game where two puppets appear and she has to pat each down. The game has evolved as her own interaction with objects is to throw them over her shoulder. She will, however, push things away and the game has developed as a way of encouraging her to show awareness that there are two items *and* to alter her response according to the number of items. In order to maximise their attractiveness, the handpuppets are a vibrant red with large eyes and each holds a set of metal castanets.

Sandy reaches out to touch puppet 1 (P1) which makes a noise and disappears below the table. She reaches out to the teacher and rocks back and forth, hand in mouth. Teacher makes puppet 2 (P2) make a sound and then disappear below the table.

Both puppets then reappear one each side of the table as before, making a noise as they appear. Sandy, hand in mouth, looks at P1 and then at P2; she pushes P2 which disappears below the table. Sandy rocks back and forth, glancing at P1, then bangs her hand up and down on the table repeatedly. She looks again at P1; she twiddles her hand. Teacher makes P1 make a noise and disappear. Sandy laughs.

Teacher says, '*Shall we make them come back again?*' They reappear, first one then the other, making a noise. Sandy looks at both puppets in turn and moves to push the second puppet down. Teacher moves the first puppet up to make a noise in Sandy's ear, then it disappears.

Both puppets reappear with noise and Sandy immediately reaches out to push P1 down, then turns to push P2 down.

Both puppets reappear, Sandy rocks back and forth – vocalises, '*eeh eeh*', looks around, hand in mouth, looks at teacher, pushes P1 then bangs hand. She reaches to where P1 disappeared then turns to P2 and pushes it down. Teacher responds '*Good girl, that was really clever.*'

Both puppets reappear making a noise. Sandy reaches towards P1 and it disappears. Sandy puts her head down on the table, moving her hand in her mouth, moves her arm up and down on the table, glancing towards the puppet, then bangs again and reaches out to push P2 down.

Table 12.2:

Task	Context	Teacher Action	Pupil Response
Respond to two items	Resources: 2 Elmo puppets holding castanets Location: Quiet room Organisation: 1:1	Presents puppets at opposite sides of table, shaking castanets as they appear P1 disappears P2 disappears	Touches P1
		Puppets reappear P2 disappears P1 disappears	Pushes P2 Looks at P1
		P1 & P2 reappear P2 disappears P1 disappears	Looks at both puppets in turn Pushes P2
		P1 & P2 reappear P1 disappears P2 disappears	Sandy pushes P1 Pushes P2
		Puppets both reappear P1 disappears P2 disappears	Sandy pushes P1 & bangs the spot Pushes P2
		Puppets both reappear P1 disappears P2 disappears	Sandy pushes P1 Head on table, bangs, glances & pushes P2

By dividing this narrative observation into episodes, it is possible to examine how often Sandy pushes both puppets down. Alternatively, we can glance at the more conventional recording of the system shown in Table 12.2. This displays clearly that on the final three occasions, Sandy touched or knocked both puppets. In the earlier instances, the teacher responds *as if* she has touched them. She does this because she wants to keep the momentum of the game. Some might argue that in doing this she does not encourage Sandy to realise that when she pushes the puppet it will go. However, it is only necessary for the teacher to do this at the beginning and it certainly does not deter Sandy from her part in the game. Remember, the actions are only indications that she has encoded the quantity of the items, there is no right or wrong action.

In evaluating this session we can say that the method does elicit Sandy's awareness of the quantity of two and her ability to use this information to shape her actions. We might also recognise from the full observation that the teacher deliberately focuses attention on the puppets rather than her role in the game. It is, therefore, the puppets who move and make noises and she keeps her interaction low key.

These vignettes serve to demonstrate that the conventional type of recording can be quite well suited to looking at the progress of the pupil *and* to evaluating this in the context of the teacher's actions including the way the task is presented. Space here does not permit comparison over time when we might, in the above example, evaluate Sandy's responses in relation to other stimuli. For example, how attentive is she to castanets on their own or the puppets on their own? In fact, for Sandy, visual stimuli are important but the sound attracts her attention and, therefore, comparisons across sessions enable us to identify the need for both. (We would, of course, also want to see how her responses vary when there is one or three items.)

Conclusion
Teaching children with complex needs is not often a straightforward task. It demands that teachers have knowledge and understanding of a whole range of teaching approaches. Teachers must have the ability and confidence to follow the child's lead as well as to use more structured approaches. In this book we have outlined a number of methods that use visual access systems to promote learning. As we argued at the outset, for many pupils, but not all, visual processes are a robust way of taking in and memorising information. The use of different methods may also help the teacher to think again about aspects of his or her teaching. Evaluation is a core element within this. It can be argued that professional development is dependent on reflection on practice and the ability to use this information to facilitate learning in those pupils with the most complex needs.

Key summary points
- Formal evaluations of these methods are limited.
- Evaluation forms a vital part of our teaching.
- We need to record pupil progress AND examine how effective our methods have been.
- Our recording systems therefore need to include information about the context of learning, actions of teachers, as well as pupil responses.
- We need to take the time to look across sessions to make comparisons.

References and useful further reading
Male, D. (1996a) 'Who goes to MLD schools?' *British Journal of Special Education*, 23, 1, 35–41.

Male, D. (1996b) 'Who goes to SLD schools?' *Journal of Applied Research in Intellectual Disabilities*, 9, 4, 307–23.

Pagliano, P. (1999) *Multisensory Environments*. London: David Fulton Publishers.